ESSENTIAL
AMSTERDAM

Original text by George McDonald
Updated by Mike Gerrard

© Automobile Association Developments Limited 2009
First published 2007
Reprinted 2009. Information verified and updated

ISBN: 978-0-7495-6002-7

Published by AA Publishing, a trading name of Automobile Association Developments
Limited, whose registered office is Fanum House, Basing View, Basingstoke,
Hampshire RG21 4EA. Registered number 1878835.

Automobile Association Developments Limited retains the copyright in the original
edition © 2000 and in all subsequent editions, reprints and amendments

A CIP catalogue record for this book is available from the British Library

Colour separation: MRM Graphics Ltd
Printed and bound in Italy by Printer Trento S.r.l.

A03616
Maps in this title produced from mapping © MAIRDUMONT / Falk Verlag 2008
Transport map © Communicarta Ltd, UK

About this book

This book is divided into six sections.

The essence of Amsterdam
pages 6–19
Introduction; Features; Food and drink;
Short break including the 10 Essentials

Planning pages 20–33
Before you go; Getting there; Getting around; Being there

Best places to see pages 34–55
The unmissable highlights of any visit to Amsterdam

Best things to do pages 56–81
Great cafés; stunning views and more

Exploring pages 82–165
The best places to visit in Amsterdam, organized by area

Excursions pages 166–183
Places to visit out of town

Maps
All map references are to the maps on the covers. For example, Begijnhof has the reference ✚ 5F – indicating the grid square in which it is to be found.

Admission prices
Inexpensive (under €5)
Moderate (€5–€7)
Expensive (€7.50–€12)
Very expensive (over €12)

Hotel prices
Price are per room per night: € budget (under €100); €€ moderate (€100–€250); €€€ expensive to luxury (over €250)

Restaurant prices
Price for a three-course meal per person without drinks: € budget (under €25); €€ moderate (€25–€50); €€€ expensive (over €50)

Contents

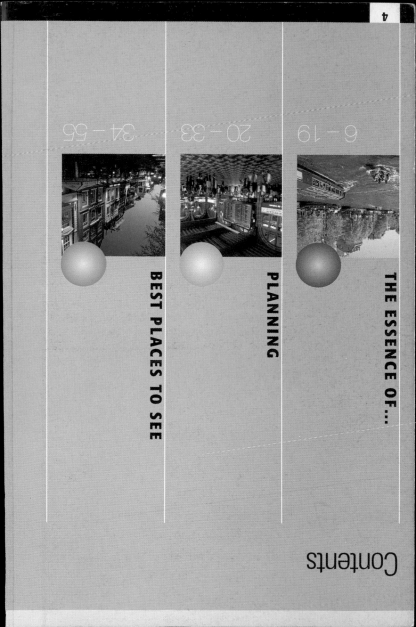

BEST THINGS TO DO

56 – 81

EXPLORING...

82 – 165

EXCURSIONS

166 – 182

The essence of...

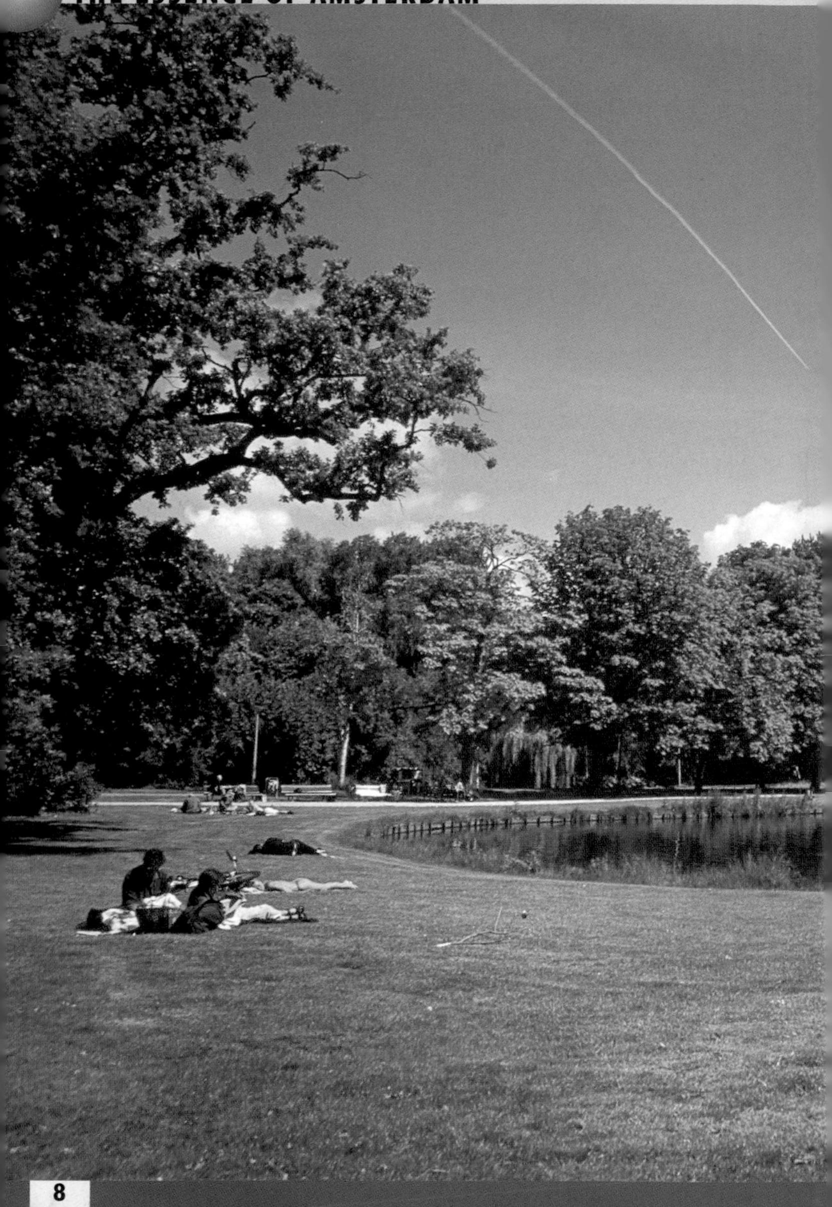

Amsterdam has two faces. First, there is the historic city, in particular its 17th-century Golden Age legacy, which you can see and touch all around you as you stroll the canalsides. There are thousands of protected monuments from this period, and if you can blot out the many contemporary distractions it's easy to imagine Rembrandt strolling there, sketchbook in hand. Then there is the modern city, which has become a byword for its famously – some would say excessively – tolerant and freewheeling lifestyle. It's a tale of two cities, but in Amsterdam it is always the best of times.

features

If this is your first visit you have a special treat in store – making the acquaintance of this beautiful and fascinating city will give you fond memories. If you've been here before, you already know something of the atmosphere here, and now you have the chance to dig deeper. Amsterdam rewards those who want to get below the surface, to get closer to the life of the city and its people.

It's hard not to be seduced by the rows of elegant, gabled, 17th-century buildings, their images reflected in the canals. Amsterdam cherishes them and makes them the stage for its own vibrant and inventive lifestyle, thereby serving up the best of both worlds. You'll have all the sonorous incantations of history, art and culture you can handle, and afterwards let your hair down and party till the sun comes up.

GEOGRAPHY

● Amsterdam stands on the southern shore of the IJsselmeer lake, formerly the Zuiderzee, 24km (15 miles) east of Holland's North Sea coast. It lies 3.3m (11ft) below mean sea-level, and is protected from flooding by strong coastal and river dikes.

● Water forms one-tenth of the city's area – 20sq km (7.8sq miles) out of 200.

SEAFOOD

Maatjes (raw herring) is a Dutch treat, bought from street stalls, served with raw onion, and eaten whole or chopped into slices. Almost as popular is *gerookte paling* (smoked eel), traditionally from the IJsselmeer. In months with an 'r' in them, you can eat *mosselen* (mussels) and *oesters* (oysters) from the waters of Zeeland's Eastern Scheldt estuary. Prawns are popular and tasty. All kinds of other fish are available, including cod, sole, plaice, turbot, salmon and halibut, as well as Mediterranean and tropical species.

INDONESIAN

The Dutch East Indies were the jewel of Holland's colonial empire. In a reversal of fortunes, Indonesian cuisine has conquered the former mother country. Highlight of the menu is *rijsttafel* (rice table), a cascade of up to 20 or more dishes ranging from mild to volcanically spicy. *Rijsttafel* was invented by the colonial Dutch, and there is a tendency to look down on it as being for tourists only, yet it provides a good introduction to Indonesian cuisine. As menus often have no English translation, look for such items as *ayam* (chicken), *ikan* (fish), *telor* (egg), *rendang* (beef), *kroepoek* (shrimp crackers), *sateh* (pork kebabs in spicy peanut sauce) and *gado-gado* (vegetables in peanut sauce).

CHEESE

Round Edam and cylindrical Gouda cheeses are the best known. Try also *Leidse kaas*, flavoured with caraway seeds, and *Friese kaas*, flavoured with cloves.

DRINKS

Dutch pilsener beers Heineken, Grolsch and Amstel are well known, and there are others, such as Oranjeboom, Bavaria, Brand, Gulpen, Ridder, Leeuw, Alfa and Lindeboom. For a change, try a *witbier* (white beer) such as Wiekse Witte, or a brown *bokbier*. Dutch *jenever* (gin), usually ordered as a *borreltje* (small tot), is a popular accompaniment to beer, the two forming a symbiotic relationship called a *kopstoot* ('knock on the head').

SNACKS

● Arguably, Dutch food is better for snacking. Street vendors offer raw herring, and, less of an acquired taste, chips, which the Dutch traditionally eat with a glob of mayonnaise. **Vleminckx,** at Voetboogstraat 33, serves the best chips in the city (crispy on the outside, fluffy on the inside). Other vendors sell Belgian waffles and pancakes; several

cafés, such as the
Pancake Bakery
(➤ 61), serve pancakes
and little else.

● If you're feeling brave
or desperate, you might
want to try a meat or
cheese-filled croquette
deep fried in
breadcrumbs from
**Febo's coin-operated
hatches**: there are
outlets of this all
over town.

● **At lunchtime**, most
Amsterdammers make
do with a *broodje*
(sandwich), either in a
café or from one of the
many take-away
sandwich shops. Cafés
also traditionally serve
bitterballen (like
croquettes but round),
uitsmijter (fried eggs on
ham and cheese and
bread), and often home-
made *appelgebak*
(apple pie), served with
a dollop of *slagroom*
(whipped cream). The
pie at the **Winkel**
(Noordermarkt 43),
heavily flavoured with
cinnamon and with the
flakiest of crusts, may
be the culinary highlight
of your stay.

short break

If you have only a short time to visit Amsterdam and would like to take home some unforgettable memories you can do something local and capture the real flavour of the city. The following suggestions will give you a wide range of sights and experiences that won't take very long, won't cost very much and will make your visit very special. If you only have time to choose just one of these, you will have found the true heart of the city.

● **Take a canal boat cruise** (➤ 70–71), the best way to view this canal-threaded city and its gabled houses; it's even better after dark, when the canals are illuminated. The best tours go clockwise and include the Amstel River – look out for sights such as the Magere Brug (➤ 133) and Amstelhof. The popular Herengracht canal borders central Amsterdam and is a favourite with visitors.

● **Rent a bicycle** and make a self-guided tour of the city the way Amsterdammers get around, or take our suggested tour (➤ 74–75). This is definitely the best way to

tour the hidden parts of the city, and bicycles are much easier to park than a car in this city of narrow streets.

● **Climb the Westerkerk tower** (➤ 55) for a great view over the *grachtengordel* (ring canals) and the Jordaan (➤ 146–147). Or, venture to the top of the tower of the Beurs van Berlage (➤ 87) which looks down on the old heart of Amsterdam.

● **Visit the Rijksmuseum** (➤ 48–49) to see Rembrandt's *The Night Watch*, the essence of the city's 17th-century Golden Age, but note that most of the museum is closed until 2010. However, the 400 or more paintings displayed as 'The Masterpieces' will satisfy most visitors until the renovation of the museum is complete.

● **Do the old centre walk** (➤ 72–73), which shows you there is more than the Red Light District to this part of town. In just 2 hours, you will see the university campus, pass merchants' houses, discover second-hand bookstalls in narrow passages and red-lit windows in the Red Light District.

● **Have a drink or dine al fresco** at an outside terrace. De Jaren (➤ 60), beside the Amstel, has a great terrace for drinks; as has Wildschut (➤ 165) in Amsterdam South. At the first hint of good weather, restaurants and cafés with outdoor terraces fill up instantly.

● **Visit a brown café** (➤ 58–59), one of the city's traditional, tobacco-stained bars, or a *proeflokaal*, an old gin-tasting house. Here you'll find an unhurried approach to life and almost a guarantee of friendly conversation.

● **Listen to buskers** (street musicians) and watch other performers – jugglers, mime artists and more – at Leidseplein (➤ 44–45), the entertainment centre.

● **Stroll through Vondelpark** (➤ 52–53) in summer for the colour and animation that light up the park when the sun shines. This is a great

place to relax away from the bustle and is popular with locals.

● **Travel on a tram** – Pick up a tram from Centraal Station (➤ 89) to take you to many of the city's top attractions. On the older trams, children can stand beside the driver.

Planning

Before you go

WHEN TO GO

JAN	FEB	MAR	APR	MAY	JUN	JUL	AUG	SEP	OCT	NOV	DEC
5°C	6°C	9°C	12°C	16°C	19°C	21°C	22°C	18°C	13°C	9°C	6°C
41°F	43°F	48°F	54°F	61°F	66°F	70°F	72°F	64°F	55°F	48°F	43°F

🌧 ❄ ☁ 🌦 ☀ ☀ ☀ ☀ 🌦 🌧 🌧 🌧

● High season ○ Low season

Temperatures are the average daily maximum for each month.

The weather in Amsterdam is generally mild. The most delightful month to visit is May, when there is less rainfall. June to August are the busiest months for visitors, although rain is likely at some times in the summer. September is also a good time with few visitors, although more rain is likely. The weather can be chilly and drizzly between October and March. There can be strong winds and fog to contend with at this time of year. However, during December, Amsterdam is popular with foreign visitors shopping for Christmas presents or spending the festive season in the city. Also during the winter, in January and February, it can be so cold that the canals freeze over. It's not surprising in a city built on water, and can be a magical time to visit, but you will need extra warm clothing.

WHAT YOU NEED

● Required ○ Suggested ▲ Not required

Some countries require a passport to remain valid for a minimum period (usually at least six months) beyond the date of entry – check before you travel.

	UK	Germany	USA	Spain
Passport (or National Identity Card where applicable)	●	●	●	●
Visa (regulations can change – check before you travel)	▲	▲	▲	▲
Onward or Return Ticket	▲	▲	▲	▲
Health Inoculations	▲	▲	▲	▲
Health Documentation (▶ 23, Health insurance)	●	●	●	●
Travel Insurance	○	○	○	○
Driving Licence (national)	●	●	●	●
Car Insurance Certificate (if own car)	○	○	○	○
Car Registration Document (if own car)	●	●	●	●

WEBSITES

Amsterdam tourist advice:
www.visitamsterdam.nl
www.amsterdam.info

www.holland.com/amsterdam
www.amsterdam.nl

TOURIST OFFICES AT HOME

In the UK
Netherlands Board of Tourism (NBT)
✉ PO Box 30783,
London WC2B 6DH
☎ 020 7539 7950;
www.holland.com/uk

In the USA
Netherlands Board of Tourism (NBT)
✉ 355 Lexington Avenue,
NY 10017

☎ 212/370-7360;
www.holland.com/us

In Canada
Netherlands Board of Tourism (NBT)
✉ 14 Glenmount Court, Whitby,
Ontario L1N 5M8
☎ 905/666-5960

HEALTH INSURANCE

EU nationals can obtain free medical treatment in the Netherlands with a European Health Insurance Card (EHIC), although 10 per cent of prescribed medicine must be paid for. Private medical insurance is still advised and is essential for all other visitors.

For urgent dental treatment, contact the Central Medical Service (tel: 0900 503 2042). Emergency treatment is available at reduced cost for citizens of the EU but costs are high and insurance is recommended, and is essential for all other visitors.

TIME DIFFERENCES

GMT	Amsterdam	Germany	USA (NY)	Spain	Australia
12 noon	1PM	1PM	7AM	1PM	10PM

Holland is on Central European Time (GMT+1). Dutch Summer Time (GMT+2) operates from late March, when clocks are put forward one hour, until late October.

NATIONAL HOLIDAYS

1 Jan *New Year's Day*
Mar/Apr *Good Friday,*
Easter Sunday,
Easter Monday
Apr/May *Ascension Day*
30 Apr *Queen's Day*

4 May *Remembrance Day*
5 May *Liberation Day*
May/Jun *Pentecost Sunday*
and Pentecost Monday
25 Dec *Christmas Day*

26 Dec *Second Day of*
Christmas

Banks, businesses, most
shops and some museums
close on these days.

WHAT'S ON WHEN

February *Pre-Lenten Carnival* (early February): Amsterdam's has had a less than chequered career, because carnival-goers prefer Maastricht's.

March *Stille Omgang* (Sunday near 15 March): Catholic procession celebrating the 1345 'Miracle of the Host'.
Keukenhof Garden (late March–late May): Beautiful gardens at Lisse open, as tulips and other spring flowers blossom.

April *National Museum Weekend* (mid-month): Free or reduced-price.
World Press Photo Awards (Monday, mid-April): Annual photojournalism prizes.
Koninginnedag (30 April): Queen Beatrix's official birthday – massive street parties and free markets.

May *Herdenkingsdag* (4 May): Remembrance Day for World War II victims; two-minute silence at 8pm.
Bevrijdingsdag (5 May): Liberation Day celebrations; a less frenetic version of Koninginnedag.
National Windmill Day (second Saturday): Windmills open.
Vlaggetjesdag (last Saturday): Flag Day fishing-boat race at Scheveningen to bring back the first new herring for the queen.

June *Amsterdam Roots Festival* (early to mid-June): Festival of world music, dance, films, exhibits and workshops, at the Melkweg multimedia cultural centre and others.
Canalhouse Gardens in Bloom (mid-June): Private canalhouse gardens on Herengracht, Keizersgracht and Prinsengracht open to the public.

Holland Festival (throughout June): International arts festival in Amsterdam, The Hague, Rotterdam and Utrecht.

July *Amsterdam Arts Adventure*: Amsterdam's main cultural season runs from September until June, which used to mean that the city was a cultural desert at the busiest time of the year for tourism. Arts Adventure fills the gap with a varied programme of mostly informal, often open-air, music, theatre and dance events from June to August. For information, contact VVV tourist offices and Amsterdam Uit Buro.
North Sea Jazz Festival: An annual three-day event at The Hague's Nederlands Congres Centrum during July is an excuse the visit the city. You'll hear many of the big international names in jazz and blues in more than a hundred concerts. Contact the organizers on 015/215 7756; ww.northseajazz.nl.

August *Amsterdam Pride*: One of the biggest gay festivals in Europe.
Prinsengracht Concert (penultimate Saturday): Pulitzer Hotel hosts classical music concert on a barge.
Uitmarkt (last weekend): Cultural venues preview the new season.

September *Open Monumentendag* (second Saturday): Monuments and buildings that are usually closed or only partly open, are open.

November *Sinterklaas* (third Saturday): Holland's Santa Claus parades through town.

December *Pakjesavond* (5 December): Traditional day for giving presents.
Oudejaarsavond (31 December): Partying in the street and fireworks.

Getting there

BY AIR

Schiphol Airport

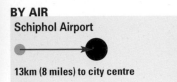

13km (8 miles) to city centre

🚆 20 minutes

🚌 30 minutes

🚗 25–30 minutes

Amsterdam has only one international airport, Schiphol (tel: 0900/0141), receiving direct flights from the US and Europe. Numerous carriers operate flights into Schiphol including British Airways, Virgin, easyJet, Air France, Air Canada and Continental. Holland's national carrier, KLM Royal Dutch Airlines (tel: 020/474 7747 in Amsterdam; 08705 074074 in the UK: 1-800-225-2525 (Northwest Airlines) in the US; www.klm.nl), has scheduled flights from Britain, Europe and beyond to Schiphol.

Approximate flying times to Amsterdam: London (1 hour); Dublin (1.5 hours); New York (7 hours); West Coast USA (10.5 hours); Vancouver (9.25 hours); Montréal (7.5 hours); Sydney (20 hours); Auckland (21.5 hours).

Schiphol airport is 13km (8 miles) southwest of Amsterdam city centre. The journey from the airport takes about 20 minutes by train and services run every 10 minutes from 6am until midnight. The cost is €3.60 and tickets must be bought in advance. Alternatively, buses run once or twice every hour between the airport and a number of large hotels. The fare is around €12.

Taxis run into Amsterdam, too, but the fares are expensive – often four or five times higher than the cost of travelling by public transport. It is

probably best to go to Centraal Station by train and continue onwards by taxi from there.

BY RAIL

Centraal Station has connections with major European cities. High-speed trains connect Amsterdam with Paris, Brussels and Cologne. Eurostar from Britain connects with Brussels and offers good fares onwards to Amsterdam. For train information (tel: 0900/9292; www.ns.nl).

BY SEA

There are ferry services between Britain and IJmuiden (23km/14 miles), Rotterdam Europoort (70km/43 miles) and Hoek van Holland (68km/ 42 miles). All have rail links to Amsterdam. Crossing time is around 3.75 hours.

Getting around

PUBLIC TRANSPORT

Internal flights Distances between Dutch cities are relatively so short that air travel is rarely worth while, but KLM subsidiaries KLM Cityhopper and KLM Exel connect Amsterdam, Eindhoven, Enschede, Groningen and Maastricht.

Trains Trains are the best way to get to many nearby destinations and for travel throughout the country. The trains are clean and the service is punctual. Intercity (IC) trains are fast (not high speed).

Trams It's hard to imagine Amsterdam without trams; its transport company, Gemeentevervoerbedrijf (GVB), runs 17 tram lines. For public transport information, call 0900 9292 or visit www.GVB.nl.

Buses GVB buses complement the tram network. Connexxion buses handle regional services; they are generally slower than trains to common destinations, but serve many places that trains don't.

Metro There are four Metro lines: 50, 51, 53 and 54. These lines serve the suburbs and are generally not useful for points within the city centre, except for Nieuwmarkt, which has no tram or bus service, Waterlooplein and Centraal Station.

Boat Most canal boats are touring rather than transport options. For that you need Canal Bus (tel: 623 9886), Museum Boat (tel: 530 1090), which connects many popular museums and other attractions, and Water Taxi (tel: 530 1090).

TAXIS

Generally you cannot hail taxis on the street, although some will stop if you do. You can pick up taxis at the airport, main railway stations, busy city locations and outside bigger hotels. To call a cab, ring Taxi Centrale (tel: 677 7777).

CAR RENTAL

The main companies have offices at Schiphol Airport and in town. Driving in Amsterdam is not recommended, as the narrow streets are congested and parking costs, and the penalties, are high.

DRIVING

- If your car breaks down, contact ANWB Wegenwacht (tel: 0800 0888). On motorways use the yellow-coloured emergency phones (every 2km/ 1 mile) to contact the emergency breakdown service.
- Drive on the right.
- Speed limits on motorways *(snelwegen)* are 100kmh (62mph) on ring roads, approaches to towns, and other busy stretches; 120kmh (74mph) on other sections; 80kmh (50mph) on country roads; and 50kmh (31mph) on urban roads.
- Seatbelts must be worn in front seats at all times and in rear seats where fitted.
- Random breath-testing takes place. Never drive under the influence of alcohol.
- Fuel *(benzine)*, is sold as Super: 98-octane leaded *(lood)*; Super plus: 98-octane unleaded *(loodvri)*; and Euro: 95-octane unleaded. Diesel and liquid petroleum gas *(autogas)* are also available.

FARES AND CONCESSIONS

General A 1-, 2- or 3- day Amsterdam Pass, available from NBT and VVV offices, allows free admission to more than 20 museums and attractions, as well as other free and discount offers, and free use of public transport.

Students/youths An inexpensive Cultureel Jongeren Pas (Cultural Youth Pass), available from VVV offices or Uit Buro (valid for a year), entitles anyone under 26 to free admission to many museums, and discounts on cultural events.

Senior citizens Many museums, attractions and performance venues have reduced admission prices for seniors.

Being there

TOURIST OFFICES
Holland Tourist Information (HTi)
Schiphol Plaza
Amsterdam Airport Schiphol
☎ 205 512525
🕐 Daily 7am–10pm

VVV (Vereniging voor Vreemdelingen Verkeer) is the name for Holland's tourist information organizations, with offices in every city and town.

VVV Amsterdam
✉ Postbus 3901
1001 AS Amsterdam
☎ 205 512525
www.visitamsterdam.nl

Centraal Station
Platform 2 & Stationsplein 10
🕐 Daily 9–5 (later during summer and other peak periods)

Leidseplein 1
🕐 Daily 9–6 (later during summer)

MONEY
The currency is the euro (€). There are banknotes for 5, 10, 20, 50, 100, 200 and 500 euros, and coins for 1, 2, 5, 10, 20 and 50 cents, and 1 and 2 euros.

Change money at banks and bureaux de change. Grenswisselkantoor (GWK), with exchange offices at Schiphol airport, Centraal Station and other main railway stations and ports offers fair deals but other bureaux de change may not. Although traveller's cheques are accepted at some hotels, restaurants and shops, it is better to change them at banks or GWK offices.

TIPS AND GRATUITIES
Yes ✓   No ✗

Hotels (service included)	✓	change
Restaurants (service included)	✓	change
Cafés/bars (service included)	✓	change
Taxis (service included)	✓	10%
Tour guides	✓	€1/€5
Porters (charge)	✓	change
Chambermaids	✓	€3/€5
Toilets	✗	

POSTAL AND INTERNET SERVICES

Old post boxes are red, but most are now orange. Most PTT post offices (*postkaanturen*) are open Monday to Friday 9–5. The Hoofdpostkantoor (head post office) is at Singel 250–256 (tel: 0900 767 8526; open Mon–Fri 9–6, Sat 10–2).

WiFi internet access is becoming increasingly common in hotels and cafés, or try Freeworld Internet Café (Kort Nieuwendijk 30, open daily 10am–midnight) and The Internet Café (Martelaarsgracht 11, open Sun–Thu 9am–1pm, Fri–Sat 9am–3pm). Rates are around €1 for 30 minutes.

TELEPHONES

Most public telephones accept KPN Telecom cards *(telefoonkaarten)* of €5, €13 and €25; some accept coins of 5, 10, 20 and 30 cents and €1 and €2; and some accept credit cards. KPN teleboutiques, post offices and newsagents sell phonecards. International operator: 0800 0410.

Emergency telephone numbers

Police, Ambulance, Fire: 112   Tourist Medical Service: 5923355

EMBASSIES

UK
Consulate ☎ 676 4343
Embassy ☎ 070/4270 427

Germany
Embassy ☎ 070/342 0600

USA
Consulate ☎ 575 5309
Embassy ☎ 070/310 9209

Spain
☎ 070/364 3814

Canada
☎ 070/311 1600

Australia
☎ 070/310 8200

HEALTH ADVICE

Sun advice Even in mid-summer, temperatures in Amsterdam rarely reach much above 25°C (77°F). If you plan to do a lot of sightseeing on foot at this time, wear sunscreen and drink plenty of fluids.
Drugs Prescription and non-prescription drugs are sold in *apotheeken* (pharmacies), recognized by a green cross sign. The addresses of

out-of-hours pharmacies are posted on pharmacy doors and windows.
Drogerijen (drug stores) only sell toiletries and cosmetics.

Safe water Tap water is safe to drink. Bottled mineral water is available.

PERSONAL SAFETY

Opportunistic theft, such as pickpocketing and stealing from distracted
people, is common and tourists are a prime target. Robbery with violence
is rarer, but take sensible precautions:

● Avoid quiet places at night, particularly if you are alone.
● Watch out for your removables on trams, at Centraal Station, Schiphol
   Airport, in museums, at markets and on the beach.
● Leave nothing visible in your car.

ELECTRICITY

The power supply is 220 volts. Sockets take two-round-pin plugs. An
adaptor is needed for most non-Continental appliances and a voltage
transformer for appliances operating on 100–120 volts; exceptions are the
shavers that use 110-volt sockets you find in many hotel rooms.

OPENING HOURS

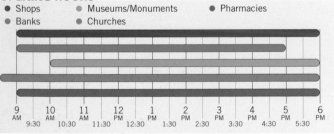

Some shops close between noon and 2pm and all day Sunday and
Monday, some open at 2pm on Monday, many stay open until 9pm.
Department stores open from noon until 5pm on Sunday. Supermarkets
open Monday to Friday from 8am until 8pm, and 6pm on Saturday. Some
food shops open from 5pm until midnight. Some banks close at 4pm,
some stay open until 7pm on Thursday, and some open on Saturday.
Government offices open Monday to Friday from 8:30am until 4pm.

LANGUAGE

Most Dutch people speak at least some English and many are fluent. This can make it frustrating if you want to practise speaking Dutch, as often a question you ask in Dutch will be answered in English. Not everybody speaks English, though, making it useful to know some Dutch words, and attempts to use them will be appreciated. The 'oo' (pronounced 'oa' as in load) and 'ee' constructions (pronounced 'ay' as in day) are particularly problematic for English-speakers and lead to common errors; as an example, remember the department store Vroom & Dreesman is pronounced 'Vrome & Drayssman'. If you pronounce 'ij' like English 'eye' you'll be close enough: for example *prijs* 'price'; *ontbijt* 'ontbite'.

yes	*ja*	sorry	*excuseer/pardon*
no	*nee*	today	*vandaag*
please	*alstublieft*	tomorrow	*morgen*
thank you	*dank u wel*	yesterday	*gisteren*
hello	*dag/hallo*	how much?	*hoeveel?*
goodbye	*dag/tot ziens*	closed	*gesloten*
goodnight	*welterusten*	open	*geopend*
hotel	*hotel*	reservation	*reservering*
room	*kamer*	breakfast	*ontbijt*
single/	*eenpersoonskamer/*	toilet	*toilet/WC*
double	*tweepersoonskamer*	bathroom	*badkamer*
one/two nights	*een/twee nachten*	shower	*douche*
per person/	*per persoon/*	room service	*room service*
bank	*bank*	traveller's cheque	*reisecheque*
credit card	*creditcard*	exchange rate	*wisselkoers*
lunch	*lunch/middageten*	drink	*drank/drankje*
dinner	*diner/avondeten*	the bill	*de rekening*
airport	*luchthaven*	single/return	*enkele reis/retour*
train	*trein*	first/second class	*eerste/tweede klas*
ferry	*veerboot*	non-smoking	*niet roken*

Best
places
to see

1 Amsterdams Historisch Museum

www.ahm.nl

A visit to this impressive museum will enrich your understanding of the city's 750-year history, adding useful insights to walks around town.

Sequential displays of art, models, maps, weapons, household objects and other artefacts trace Amsterdam's development from fishing village to trading post, pilgrimage centre, seapower and Golden Age capital; through wars, religious strife, decline and renewal, to today's vibrant metropolis. There are archaeological finds from the city's earliest days, the oldest city map, *Bird's Eye View of Amsterdam* by Cornelis Anthoniszoon (1538), four beautiful late 15th-century altar cushions depicting the *Miracle of the Host* in 1345, maps

and globes by Johannes Blaeu, and the Schuttersgalerij (➤ 106), a corridor lined with Civic Guard paintings.

The Historical Museum opened in 1975 in the former Burgerweeshuis (City Orphanage), which took over the Sint-Luciënklooster, a 15th-century convent, after the 1578 Protestant Alteration. Architect Hendrick de Keyser added a new wing in 1598 and in 1632 his son Pieter built the Renaissance colonnade you see lining a courtyard shaded by a lime tree planted for Queen Wilhelmina's 1898 coronation. In 1634, the old convent was demolished and Jacob van Campen began construction of the main orphanage building. The museum has been renovated and uses interactive media to focus on the growth of Amsterdam and specific periods in its history.

Among the 17th-century Golden Age paintings, you can see the remains of Rembrandt's fire-damaged *The Anatomy Lesson of Dr Deijman*; Willem van de Velde the Younger's *The River IJ at Amsterdam*; Gerard de Lairesse's T*he Continents Paying Homage to the Maid of Amsterdam*; and Hendrick Corneliszoon Vroom's *The Return to Amsterdam of the Second Expedition to the Indies*, an event that greatly boosted the city's wealth.

➕ 5F ✉ Kalverstraat 92, Nieuwezijds Voorburgwal 357, Sint-Luciënsteeg 27 ☎ 523 1822 🕐 Mon–Fri 10–5, Sat–Sun and public hols 11–5. Closed 1 Jan, 30 Apr, 25 Dec 💶 Moderate 🍴 David and Goliath Café (€€) 🚊 1, 2, 4, 5, 6, 9, 14, 16, 24, 25 🚢 Museum Boat stop 4 ❓ Guided tours on request; call ahead ~~amsterdamCard free adult 10 euro~~

2 Anne Frank Huis

www.annefrank.nl

Anne Frank wrote her famous diary in a secret annexe of this canal house, where she and her family hid from Nazi persecution.

In July 1942, when the Germans began deporting Amsterdam's Jewish residents to concentration camps, Otto Frank, his wife, two daughters and four friends, moved into hiding in the back of this house. Anne, who was 13, began recording her thoughts in a diary. For more than two years the eight *onderduikers* ('divers' – because they dived out of sight) lived in fear and nearly total silence until, in August 1944, an informant betrayed them. Anne and her sister were sent to Bergen-Belsen, where both died of typhus early in 1945.

More than half a million visitors a year climb the narrow stairway and

pass the revolving bookcase that conceals the entrance to the bare and gloomy refuge. Its emptiness adds poignancy to simple mementoes on the walls: magazine pictures of Anne's favourite actress, Deanna Durbin, and Britain's Princesses Elizabeth and Margaret; pencilled lines marking the children's growth; a map showing the Allied advance from Normandy. Downstairs, the Anne Frank Foundation mounts exhibitions putting the diary into context. At No 265 is a wing for temporary exhibitions.

Anne hoped to publish a book about her experiences, using the diary as a basis. On 11 May 1944, she wrote: 'My greatest wish is to be a famous writer.' When Otto, the only survivor, returned after the war, a Dutch woman who had gathered up its scattered pages gave him Anne's diary. He published it in 1947 as *Het Achterhuis (The Annexe)*. Since then, *The Diary of Anne Frank* has sold more than 14 million copies in some 60 languages.

✚ 4D ✉ Prinsengracht 267 ☎ 556 7105
🕐 Mid-Mar to mid-Sep daily 9–9; mid-Sep to mid-Mar daily 9–7. Closed Yom Kippur
✋ Expensive 🍴 Café (€) 🚌 13, 17
🚢 Museum Boat stop 7 ❓ A 5-minute introductory film. The museum is generally quieter in the evening during the summer

3 Begijnhof ✗ free

www.begijnhofamsterdam.nl

A relic of Amsterdam's Catholic period, this secluded 14th-century refuge for pious women is an oasis of serenity in the heart of the city.

Begijnen (beguines) were not nuns but religious women who chose a less austere way of life, caring for poor and sick people. Most of their houses, with private gardens clustered around a tranquil walled courtyard, date from the 16th to the 18th century, all but one of the earlier wooden houses having succumbed to fire during the 15th century.

The exception is No 34, Het Houten Huys (The Wooden House) which dates from around 1425. Restored in 1957 and oldest of the city's two surviving wooden houses (the other, 't Aepje at Zeedijk 1, dates from 1550), it is now the Begijnhof information centre. Look for a courtyard beside Het Houten Huys, whose walls are dotted with gable stones salvaged from Begijnhof houses that have been demolished.

The church in the courtyard, built in 1419, was the beguines' church until Amsterdam's 1578 Protestant Alteration. Although called the Engelse Kerk (English Church), it is a Scottish Presbyterian church, having been donated to Scots' exiled in 1607. Piet Mondrian, co-founder of the De Stijl movement, created its pulpit panels, and it is still in use as a venue for church music and recitals. The

Calvinist authorities allowed the women to continue living in the Begijnhof; from 1671 until 1795 they worshipped secretly – it was an open secret – in the Mirakelkapel (Miracle Chapel) at No 31.

The last beguine died in 1971 and low-income female senior citizens now occupy the neat little houses. This is not a museum; it is their home. You should not enter after sunset or make noise or cause disturbance at any time.

🚇 5F ✉ Gedempte Begijnensloot (at Spui) 🕐 Mon–Fri 9–6, Sat–Sun 9–5 ✋ Free 🚌 1, 2, 5 ⛴ Museum Boat stop 4 ❓ Guided tours with loud commentary not allowed

4 Koninklijk Paleis

www.koninklijkhuis.nl

Constantijn Huygens called it the 'Eighth Wonder of the World', and this 17th-century structure remains the city's grandest secular building.

Jacob van Campen won the commission in 1648 to replace Dam Square's dilapidated 14th-century town hall (Stadhuis) with a new one worthy of a prosperous city. He designed a vast, soberly classical stone exterior, a novel departure from the Dutch Renaissance style, and flaunted the city's wealth in the interior with lavish amounts of Italian marble. Completed in 1655, it rests on 13,659 wooden piles.

Royalty took over in 1808 when Louis Napoleon, whose brother, the French Emperor Napoleon Bonaparte, had proclaimed him to be King of Holland two years earlier, chose the town hall for his royal palace and furnished it in Empire style. When the French left in 1813, the palace became the Amsterdam residence of the House of Orange

and is still the country's official Royal Palace.

On the pediment overlooking the Dam, Flemish sculptor Artus Quellin (1609–98) carved a baroque hymn in stone to Amsterdam's maritime pre-eminence, showing figures symbolising the oceans paying the city homage, surmounted by sculptures of Prudence, Justice and Peace. The weathervane on the cupola takes the form of a Dutch sailing ship.

Symbolism is used prodigally inside, too. In the Vierschaar (Tribunal), magistrates pronounced death sentences watched over by images of Justice, Wisdom and Mercy. Atlas struggles to hold up the globe in the Burgerzaal (Citizen's Chamber) and maps inlaid on the marble floor depict Amsterdam as centre of the world. The Schepenzaal (Council Chamber), where the aldermen met, has a painting of *Moses the Lawgiver* by Ferdinand Bol, a pupil of Rembrandt.

➕ 5E ✉ Dam ☎ 620 4060 🕐 May be closed for renovations; call or check website for latest information
🚌 1, 2, 4, 5, 6, 9, 13, 14, 16, 17, 24, 25

5 Leidseplein

www.channels.nl/leidseplein.html

What the city's liveliest square lacks in cool sophistication – and it lacks a lot – it makes up for in frenetic activity and tacky charm.

In summer, sun-worshippers, people-watchers and imbibers pack the tree-shaded café terraces rimming this busy traffic intersection. Buskers (street musicians) work the crowd, most so bad their victims gladly pay up to have them move along. Throw in the city's biggest smoking coffee shop, a plethora of restaurants, multi-screen cinemas, theatres and clubs, and you have the ingredients of a hot and spicy, non-stop entertainment centre.

A gateway in the 15th-century city wall once stood here, at the end of the road from Leiden, where wagons unloaded goods for the city. A row of 18th- and 19th-century gabled houses on the north side is now occupied by cafés and restaurants. The Stadsschouwburg (Municipal Theatre) opened in 1894, and the American Hotel, Willem Kromhout's extravagant mix of Venetian Gothic and art nouveau, noted for its art deco Café Américain, in 1902.

A sculpture called *Adamant*, by Joost van Santen (1986), in the Leidsebos (Leidse Wood) beside the Singelgracht canal,

commemorates 400 years of diamond trading in Amsterdam. You can play open-air chess on piazza-style Max Euweplein (➤ 67), an extension of Leidseplein, and try your luck at the Holland Casino Amsterdam, the city's only legal casino. Rederij Noord-Zuid canal boats and Canal Bike have moorings on Singelgracht, making getting to Leidseplein by water easy.

✚ 16H 🍴 Café Américain (€€, ➤ 60); many restaurants and cafés (€–€€€) 🚌 1, 2, 5, 6, 7, 10, 20 🚢 Museum Boat stop 5

6 Red Light District ✓ Nieuwmarkt

It's misleading to think of this as no more than one big erogenous zone. The city's oldest quarter has some surprisingly attractive canalside scenery.

Amsterdammers call this part of town De Wallen (The Walls), after the city walls that once stood here. Its two canals, Oudezijds Voorburgwal and Oudezijds Achterburgwal, are lined with lovely 16th- and 17th-century houses, many of them put to uses their Calvinist builders would find reprehensible.

The Red Light District centres most of the city's prostitution in one area where it can be controlled, and participants' health and safety more or less assured. Tourism, the international sex industry and Amsterdam's tolerant stance on drugs have transformed De Wallen, but people still live here, go shopping, walk the dog, dine out. Amid the sleaze are some good cafés and restaurants.

Few tourists visit to view the quaint gables, historic churches and second-hand bookshops, yet many tour the district not to sample its multifarious 'wares' but to experience a few harmless visual thrills before heading back to the real world. Even dedicated culture hounds will be hard put to miss the scantily clad women posing behind their red-fringed windows, although the city authorities are currently campaigning to turn some of these

into rather more conventional shopfronts. Do not attempt to photograph the women – both they and their minders are likely to react strongly to this.

Their highly personal services complement a slew of 'live shows', peep-shows, massage parlours, video libraries, and specialized book, clothing and appliance shops. Ironically, the setting can be delightful at night, when the colourful neon glows like Japanese lanterns on the inky canal surface.

✠ 6E ✉ Between Warmoesstraat, Zeedijk, Nieuwmarkt, Kloveniersburgwal and Damstraat 🍴 Many choices (€–€€) 🚇 Nieuwmarkt 🚊 4, 9, 14, 16, 24, 25 ❓ For a behind-the-scenes tour contact Rob van der Hulst Producties (www.redlight-tours.com)

7 Rijksmuseum

www.rijksmuseum.nl

For all its current truncated state, Holland's most important museum still displays the best of art from the country's 17th-century Golden Age.

Even when the State Museum was fully open, only a fraction of its 7 million-item collection was on display, ranging from the world's most important array of Dutch Golden Age art, through beautifully detailed model sailing ships to 18th-century doll's houses. Now that most of its 260 rooms are closed for renovation, you will have to settle for 'just' *The Masterpieces*, on display in the Philips Wing. But these 400 paintings and other items add up to a remarkable cultural feast.

Architect Petrus Josephus Hubertus Cuypers (1827–1921) designed the building as a neo-Renaissance palace; as construction (1865–85) proceeded, he added neo-Gothic elements.

Rembrandt's masterpiece *The Company of Captain Frans Banning Cocq and Lieutenant Willem van Ruytenburch*, better known as *The Night Watch* (1642), is the star. There are a number of other Rembrandts held here.

The wealth of emblematic paintings by leading artists is stunning: Jan Steen; Frans Hals; Willem van de Velde the Elder; Pieter Saenredam; Hendrick Averkamp; Jacob van Ruisdael; and Karel Dujardin. Jan Vermeer (1632–75) is represented by four works: *The Milkmaid* (1658), *The Little Street* (c1658), *The Love Letter* (c1670) and *Woman Reading a Letter* (1662–63).

Apart from the paintings, there's the china and porcelain collection, which includes a magnificent assortment of blue and polychrome Delftware; and some of the museum's prints and engravings.

The Rijksmuseum's garden is a restful scene, and the setting for a collection of sculptural fragments, including the Fragments Building, a mishmash of pilasters, gables, lion masks and festoons from demolished monuments. A temporary structure houses the Infocentrum Het Rijksmuseum (New Rijksmuseum Information Centre) which explains the renovations.

➕ 16J ✉ Philips Wing, Jan Luijkenstraat 1 ☎ 647 7000
🕐 Daily 9–6 (Fri till 10pm). Closed 1 Jan. Information Centre: daily 11–5 💶 Expensive (garden and information centre free) 🚊 2, 5 ⛴ Museum Boat stop 6

=C11
Ams Card free

8 Van Gogh Museum

www.vangoghmuseum.nl

Few artists' lives and achievements provoke such passion as those of Van Gogh (1853–90). See why, at the world's largest collection of his work.

This is home to more than 200 Van Gogh paintings, 500 drawings, seven sketchbooks, 850 letters – including the correspondence with his brother Theo – and Vincent's Japanese print collection, though not all are on permanent display. One hundred of the artist's most important works, displayed chronologically, make it possible to follow his ten-year artistic odyssey that ended in suicide. Sombre early works from Holland and Belgium give way to experiments with colour and technique in Paris, swirling colour and light from Provence, and his anguished work, *Wheatfield With Crows* (1890), painted a few days before he shot himself at the age of 37.

Other canvases on display include *The Potato Eaters* (1885); *Woman in the Café Le Tambourin* (1887); *The Yellow House* (1888), depicting the house at Arles in which Vincent stayed with Paul Gauguin; *Sunflowers* (1888); and *Branches*

With Almond Blossom (1890), sent to Theo on the birth of his son. You can also see paintings by Toulouse-Lautrec, Gauguin and other artists from the period between 1840 and 1920.

Gerrit Rietveld (1888–1964), an exponent of the De Stijl school of art, designed the museum, which opened in 1973. A dull, concrete exterior hides a bright, glass-roofed atrium that runs the four-floor building's full height and floods its exhibition areas with light. Built to accommodate 60,000 visitors a year, the museum now hosts around a million.

Temporary exhibitions are mounted in the ellipse-shaped extension by Japanese architect Kisho Kurokawa.

➕ 15K ✉ Paulus Potterstraat 7 ☎ 570 5200 🕐 Daily 10–6 (Fri till 10pm). Closed 1 Jan 🎫 Expensive 🍴 Self-service restaurant (€–€€) 🚊 2, 3, 5, 12, 16 🚤 Museum Boat stop 6 ❓ Audio-tour

€12.50

emd. Cord
are

51

9 Vondelpark ✓

www.amsterdam.info/parks

Cool place on a hot day, the city's green and scented fresh-air store is where Amsterdammers cast off those few inhibitions they have left.

The park retains much of the raffish air it acquired during the 1960s and 1970s, when it was the hippies' Amsterdam *pied à terre*. You can still see the occasional ageing hippie, though nowadays you're more likely to encounter in-line skaters and joggers in Dayglo outfits, along with walkers, sunbathers, cyclists and horseback-riders. On a 'quiet' summer walk you're liable to be pelted with frisbees, handballs, footballs, baseballs, basketballs, cricket balls and tennis balls. Assorted performance artists keep things from getting dull – everyone from the Royal Concertgebouw Orchestra to stiltwalkers, taking in mime artists and poets, fire-eaters and jugglers, theatre and dance troupes, rock 'n' roll and jazz bands along the way.

Father and son architects J D and L P Zocher laid out and landscaped the park in the 'natural' English style during the 1860s and 1870s. Named after Amsterdam's best-known poet and dramatist, Joost van den Vondel (1587–1679), the park covers 48ha (118 acres) with lawns, ornamental lakes, flowers, plants and 120 varieties of tree. Elegant turn-of-the-century town houses and villas border it, and there is both a 19th-century and a 1930s café – neither of which sell the *very* special 'gateau' (drug cake) that goes under the name 'space cake' at unofficial pathside stalls.

✚ 13K ✉ Between Stadhouderskade and Amstelveenseweg ⊕ Daily dawn–dusk 🖐 Free 🍴 Vertigo (€€, ➤ 61), Het Blauwe Theehuis (€) 🚌 1, 2, 3, 5, 6, 12, 20, 56 ⛴ Museum Boat stop 4 ❓ Open-air summer festival of concerts and theatre

10 Westerkerk ✓ free

www.westerkerk.nl

Westerkerk is one of four great churches in the city that symbolize Calvinism's triumph over Catholicism, as well as Amsterdam's Golden Age.

Unlike some historic Amsterdam churches, the grand Dutch Renaissance West Church is still in use for services. Its vast, plainly decorated nave, with wooden barrel vaulting and 12 chandeliers, is Holland's largest. The Hemony organ, finally added in 1687 after arguments about the place of music in services, has decorative panels painted by Gerard de Lairesse. Rembrandt and his son Titus were buried here in unknown graves; a memorial to the artist, attached to a pillar in 1906, was copied from a memorial stone visible in *The Night Watch*.

Work on the church began in 1620 under architect Hendrick de Keyser. When he died the following year, his son Pieter took over, and the church opened on Whit Sunday in 1631. Renovation work between 1985 and 1990

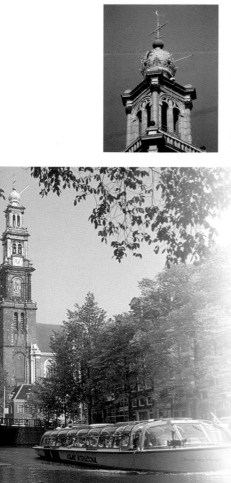

removed centuries of grime, restoring the brick and stone to their original colour.

In summer you can climb the 85m-high (279ft) Westertoren bell tower that was completed in 1638 – the city's tallest, popularly called 'Lange Jan' (Long John). A spectacular view of the canal-threaded city centre and the Jordaan is your reward. A gold, red and blue Habsburg imperial crown caps the tower, an emblem that in 1489 Maximilian of Austria gave Amsterdam the right to bear on its coat of arms. Listening to the church bells consoled Anne Frank while she hid from the Nazis, and they ring out in an hour-long carillon concert every Tuesday at noon.

The house where French philosopher René Descartes lived from 1629 till 1635, while writing his *Treatise on the Passions of the Soul*, is at Westermarkt 6.

✚ 4E ✉ Prinsengracht 281 ☎ 624 7766 🌐 Church: Apr–Sep Mon–Fri 11–3; tower 10–5 ✋ Church free; tower moderate 🚊 6, 13, 14, 17 🚤 Museum Boat stop 7

Best things to do

Brown cafés

De Druif
Nautically themed waterfront bar from 1631 in the Eastern Dock area. The cluttered interior is mainly a locals' hangout.
✉ Rapenburgerplein 83 ☎ 624 4530 🚌 Bus 22

De Engelbewaarder
Jazz on Sunday from 4pm livens up a usually tranquil, arty hang-out. This is a long narrow room with yellow half-panelled walls.
✉ Kloveniersburgwal 59 ☎ 625 3772 🚇 Nieuwmarkt 🚌 4, 9, 14, 16, 24, 25

Hoppe
Standing room only in this convivial brown café when young professionals and barfly academics drop in for a quick one, or two, after work. The building is said to date from 1670 and has sawdust on the floor and old wooden furniture in the older part. The terrace overlooks Spui square. Waiters deliver your drinks and if you are hungry, there is a small choice of soup, sandwiches and snacks.
✉ Spuistraat 18–20 ☎ 420 4420 🚌 1, 2, 5

De Karpershoek
Doesn't seem to have changed much since opening in 1629, when its customers were herring packers, sailors and dockers, and the floor is still covered with sand as it was when it first opened.
✉ Martelaarsgracht 2 ☎ 624 7886 🚌 1, 2, 5, 6, 13, 17

't Loosje

Turn-of-the-19th-century bar that used to be a horse-drawn tram waiting room. Now it is an appealing and popular venue with outside tables too. One main feature of the decoration is some wonderful tile pictures.

✉ Nieuwmarkt 32–34 ☎ 627 2635 🚇 Nieuwmarkt

Papeneiland

Traditional Amsterdam café, seemingly unchanged since 1642. It's one of the oldest brown cafés in the city. Panelled walls, Delft tiles on the walls, and a wood-burning stove add to the atmosphere.

✉ Prinsengracht 2 ☎ 624 1989 🚌 1, 2, 5, 6, 13, 17

De Reiger

Artists and students are the main customers of this restful Jordaan watering-hole.

✉ Nieuwe Leliestraat 34 ☎ 624 7426 🚌 10, 13, 14, 17

Reijnders

Traditional café on Leidseplein, a square where antique charm has mostly given way to modern frenzy.

✉ Leidseplein 6 ☎ 623 4419 🚌 1, 2, 5, 6, 7, 10

't Smalle

Originally a *proeflokaal* (tasting house), this cosy split-level café has a terrace right on the canal. Wood panelling, stained glass from the 18th century and candles on the bar complete the quaint look here. Snacks include traditional apple pie.

✉ Egelantiersgracht 12 ☎ 623 9617 🚌 13, 14, 17

De Tuin

A classic brown café in the Jordaan, with a very cosy atmosphere. The bar wears its age with pride and is popular with young people.

✉ 2e Tuinwarstraat 13 ☎ 624 4559 🚌 3, 10

Great places to have lunch

Café Américain (€€)

Popularity with tourists has slightly dimmed the cachet of this art deco café, but the continental cuisine remains good. Range of meals from snacks, through afternoon tea, to a full meal.

✉ American Hotel, Leidseplein 26 ☎ 556 3232 ⏲ Daily 7am–1am 🚊 1, 2, 5, 6, 7, 10

Café Roux (€€)

French cuisine in an elegant art nouveau setting that used to be the old town hall's canteen. A Karel Appel mural, *Inquisitive Children* (1949), is a proud fixture.

✉ Grand Hotel, Oudezijds Voorburgwal 197 ☎ 555 3560 ⏲ Daily noon–6 🚊 4, 9, 14, 16, 24, 25

Excelsior (€€€)

Haunt of celebrities, this superior restaurant beside the Amstel matches top-flight continental cuisine with good looks. Consider the fixed-price menus for more affordable dining. Unusually for Amsterdam, but understandably, formal attire is required.

✉ Hôtel de l'Europe, Nieuwe Doelenstraat 2–8 ☎ 531 1777 ⏲ Daily 7am–11am, 6pm–11pm, also Mon–Fri 12:30–2:30 🚊 4, 9, 14, 24, 25

De Jaren (€–€€)

Trendy grand café in a vast, remodelled bank, serving drinks and snacks downstairs and Dutch and continental food upstairs. The Amstel waterfront terraces are a big draw.

✉ Nieuwe Doelenstraat 20–22 ☎ 625 5771 ⏲ Sun–Thu 10am–1am, Fri–Sat 10am–2am 🚊 4, 9, 16, 24, 25

De Kas (€€€)

This out-of-the-way eatery in a 1926 greenhouse is *the* place for trendy locals. The international dishes have a Mediterranean slant.

✉ Kamerlingh Onneslaan 3 ☎ 462 4562 ⏲ Mon–Fri 12–2, 6:30–10, Sat 6:30–10 🚊 9

Luxembourg (€)

Grand café where the club sandwiches are renowned and specials include dim sum and Indonesian snacks.

✉ Spuistraat 22–24

☎ 620 6264 🕔 Sun–Fri 9am–1am, Fri–Sat 9am–2am 🚊 1, 2, 5

✓ Pancake Bakery (€)

Traditional and inventive pancakes – more than 50 on the menu. Fillings are savoury or sweet; jam and butterscotch are in pots on each table. In the basement of an old canal house.

✉ Prinsengracht 191 ☎ 625 1333 🕔 Daily noon–9:30 🚊 13, 14, 17

La Rive (€€€)

High-end French cuisine with a light, modern touch delivered in a plush and formal Michelin-rated *salle* overlooking the Amstel.

✉ Amstel InterContinental Hotel, Professor Tulpplein 1 ☎ 520 3264

🕔 Mon–Fri lunch, Mon–Sat dinner. Closed Sat–Sun lunch, Sun dinner

🚊 6, 7, 10

Royal Café de Kroon (€€)

Turn-of-the-20th century grand café, which closed during the 1960s and reopened to acclaim during the 1990s. Order from an eclectic world menu and sit in the almost harshly modern designer interior or on an enclosed balcony overlooking the square.

✉ Rembrandtplein 17 ☎ 625 2011 🕔 Daily 10am–1am (Fri–Sat 2am)

🚊 4, 9, 14, 20

Vertigo (€€)

Brown café setting. Dishes often reflect themes from the adjacent Film Museum. The terrace is one of the best in town.

✉ Vondelpark 3 ☎ 612 3021 🕔 Daily 10am–1am 🚊 1, 2, 3, 5, 6, 12

Best views

- Beurs van Beurlage (➤ 87)

- Herengracht bridge at Thorbeckeplein (➤ 70–71)

- IJ ferry (➤ 92–93)

- Le Ciel Bleu restaurant, Hotel Okura Amsterdam, Ferdinand Bolstraat 333

- Magere Brug (➤ 133)

- Café at Metz & Co (➤ 152)

- Pakhuis café, Oostelijke Handelskade 15–17

- Terrace at NEMO (➤ 100)

- Westertoren (➤ 55)

- Zuidertoren (➤ 114)

Activities and sport

FITNESS CENTRES
These two fitness centres have gym, sauna, solarium and aerobics classes.
Fitness Aerobic Center Jansen
✉ Rokin 109–11 ☎ 626 9366 🕐 Mon–Fri 10am–10:30pm, Sat–Sun 12–8 🚋 4, 9, 14, 16, 24, 25
A Bigger Splash
✉ Looiersgracht 26–30 ☎ 624 8404
🕐 7am–midnight 🚋 7, 10

GOLF
Golfbaan Waterland
An 18-hole course in Amsterdam-Noord.
✉ Buikslotermeerdijk 141 ☎ 636 1010 🚌 Bus 30

HORSE-RIDING
Amsterdamse Manege
Out-of-town riding school.
✉ Nieuwe Kalfjeslaan 25, Amsterdamse Bos
☎ 643 1342 🚌 Bus 170, 171, 172
Hollandsche Manege
Opened in 1882 and inspired by Vienna's Spanish Riding School.
✉ Vondelstraat 140 ☎ 618 0942 🚋 1, 6

ICE-SKATING
Jaap Eden Baan
Canals can freeze in winter, turning the waterways into a skating rink. Otherwise, this is a big outdoor circuit, with a side area for beginners.
✉ Radioweg 64 ☎ 694 9652 🚋 9

SOCCER
Ajax
Amsterdam's crack soccer squad plays at a superb new stadium in Amsterdam Zuidoost.

✉ Amsterdam ArenA, ArenA Boulevard ☎ 311 1444

Ⓜ Bijlmer/ArenA

SWIMMING
De Mirandabad
Clear-roofed building with wave machines, slides and other amenities.

✉ De Mirandalaan 9 ☎ 546 4444

🚌 25

Zuiderbad
Indoor pool near the Rijksmuseum.

✉ Hobbemastraat 26 ☎ 678 1390

🚌 2, 5

TENNIS
AmstelparkTenniscentrum
Plenty of choice, with 42 outdoor and 10 indoor courts. All the outdoor ones are floodlit and available for night play.

✉ Koenenkade 8, Amsterdamse Bos

☎ 301 0700 🚌 Bus 170, 171, 172

Places to take the children

Archeon
Step into the past at this archaeological theme park between Amsterdam and Rotterdam, which re-creates scenes from Stone Age, Roman and medieval life, and tells the story of the Earth.
✉ Archeonlaan 1, Alphen aan den Rijn ☎ 0172/447 744; www.archeon.nl
🕐 Jul–Aug daily 10–6; May–Jun, Sep–Oct Tue–Sun 10–5 ✋ Very expensive
🚊 Alphen aan de Rijn

Circus Elleboog
Children learn tightrope walking, juggling and other circus tricks.
✉ Passeerdersgracht 32 ☎ 626 9370; www.elleboog.nl 🕐 Times vary, phone for details ✋ Expensive 🚌 7, 10

Dolfinarium Harderwijk
Fabulous open-air shows, and a centre for sick or injured creatures. There are also tanks where you can view the dolfins underwater.
✉ Strandboulevard Oost 1, Harderwijk ☎ 0341/467 467;
www.dolfinarium.nl 🕐 Jul–Aug daily 10–6; mid-Feb to Jun, Sep–Oct daily 10–5 ✋ Very expensive 🚊 Harderwijk

De Efteling
Near Den Bosch, this is one of Europe's oldest theme parks.
✉ Europalaan 1, Kaatsheuvel ☎ 0416/288 111; www.efteling.nl ⏰ Apr–Oct daily 10–6 (mid-Jul to end Aug Sun–Fri till 9pm, Sat till midnight) ✋ Very expensive

Kinderboerderij de Pijp
Children's farm with goats, a cow, a donkey and chickens.
✉ Lizzy Ansinghstraat 82 ☎ 664 8303 ⏰ Mon–Fri 11–5, Sat–Sun 1–5 ✋ Moderate 🚌 12, 25

Kinderkookkafé
Children aged 5 to 12 cook, serve and eat at small tables.
✉ Overtoom 325/Vondelpark 66 ☎ 625 3257; www.kinderkookkafe.nl ⏰ Sat: cooking at 3:30–6, dinner at 6–8 (age 8+); Sun cooking at 12:30–5, high tea 5–6 (age 5+); Mon–Fri 9–5 🚌 1, 2, 3, 5, 6, 12

De Krakeling Theater
Mime and puppet shows.
✉ Nieuwe Passeerdersstraat 1 ☎ 624 5123 ⏰ Phone for show times 🚌 7, 10

Madame Tussaud
Wax models, from Rembrandt to present-day heroes (➤ 96).
✉ Dam 20 ☎ 523 0623 ⏰ Daily 10–5:30 (occasionally till 9pm) ✋ Expensive 🚌 4, 9, 14, 16, 24, 25

Open-air chess
Chess played with big plastic pieces off Leidseplein.
✉ Max Euweplein

Tun Fun
A big, multi-attraction indoor play park near Waterlooplein.
✉ Mr Visserplein 7 ☎ 689 4300; www.tunfun.nl ⏰ Daily 10–6 ✋ Moderate 🚊 Waterlooplein

Markets

Albert Cuypmarkt
The city's biggest and most colourful street market: a long double row of stalls selling foodstuffs, clothes, flowers, cakes and biscuits, household goods and more.
✉ Albert Cuypstraat ⏱ Mon–Sat 9:30–5 🚊 4, 16, 24, 25

Antiek De Looier
A covered market specializing in antiques, jewellery and silverware as well as general goods.
✉ Elandsgracht 109 ⏱ Sat–Thu 11–5 🚊 7, 10, 17, 20

Bloemenmarkt
Amsterdam's famous floating Flower Market, on a line of barges beside Muntplein (➤ 88–89).
✉ Singel ⏱ Mon–Fri 9–6, Sat 9–5 🚌 4, 9, 14, 16, 24, 25

Boerenmarkt
Saturday Farmer's Market selling organic produce, bread and cheese, and New Age jewellery, scents and healthcare products.
✉ Noordermarkt ⏱ Sat 9–4 (3 in winter) 🚊 1, 2, 5, 6, 13, 17

Dappermarkt
The cheapest market in the city selling food and clothes.
✉ Dapperstraat ⏱ Mon–Sat 🚊 9, 14

Kunstmarkt Thorbeckeplein

Bijou paintings, pottery and sculpture at an elegant little Sunday art market.

✉ Thorbeckeplein ⏰ Mar–Nov Sun 10:30–6
🚌 4, 9, 14

Noordermarkt

A picturesque flea market with a wide range of goods on offer. Rummage through clothes and books and investigate the unusual offerings, including flags and statuary.

✉ Noordermarkt ⏰ Mon–Fri 9–1 🚌 1, 2, 5, 13, 17

Poszegelmarkt

Coins, medals and stamps are on sale here at this specialist market.

✉ Nieuwezijds Voorburgwal 280 ⏰ Wed, Sat 11–4
🚌 1, 2, 5, 13, 17, 20

Waterlooplein Fleemarkt

Once a standby of the city's Jewish community,
this big flea market is sure to have something of interest.

✉ Waterlooplein ⏰ Mon–Fri 9–5, Sat 8:30–5:30
🚇 Waterlooplein 🚌 9, 14

Westermarkt

Similar to the Albert Cuypmarkt (➤ opposite), but on a more intimate scale.

✉ Westerstraat ⏰ Mon–Sat 9–5
🚌 1, 2, 5, 6, 13, 17

Canals and waterways

AMSTEL

Amsterdam's river flows south to north into the city. The stretch from Utrechtsebrug to the Blauwbrug (Blue Bridge), lined with houseboats, theatres, cafés and riverside homes, presents a busy scene of canal barges, tour boats and private boats travelling up- and downriver.

AMSTERDAM-RHINE

A key waterway that stretches from the IJ to the Rhine river at Tiel, carrying mostly goods and is thought to be Europe's busiest canal.

BROUWERSGRACHT

The 'Brewers' Canal' owes its name to its 16th- and 17th-century brewery *pakhuizen* (warehouses), many now chic apartments. Attractively restored, De Kroon (The Crown) at No 118, and the modern Blauwe Burgt apartment block show how old and new are trying to live in harmony.

GROENBURGWAL

A pretty canal near the Muziektheater with gabled houses lining the route.

HERENGRACHT

Four hundred buildings along this historic 2.3km (1.5-mile) canal are protected monuments. Gentlemen's Canal, begun in 1609, was a better address than the contemporaneous Keizersgracht and Prinsengracht. The higher you progress in house numbers, the more ostentatious are the mansions, until you reach the Golden Bend, between Leidsestraat and Vijzelstraat.

Highlights of Herengracht's horseshoe-shaped course through the city are its oldest warehouses at Nos 43–45, from around 1600; Theatermuseum at Nos 168–172 (► 149); Bijbels Museum at No 366–368 (► 142–143); matching neck-gabled houses, the 'twin sisters', at Nos 390–392 and 'twin brothers' at Nos 409–411; the Jewel of Canal Houses at No 475; Kattenkabinet (Cat Museum) at No 497; the mayor's residence at No 502; and Museum Willet-Holthuysen at No 605 (➤ 98–99).

THE IJ

Amsterdam stands at the confluence of the IJ and the Amstel. In the 17th century when Amsterdam was a major maritime trading city, the IJ was at the centre of nautical activity. With the move of most maritime traffic to the North Sea Canal the business of the IJ moved to pleasure craft and shuttle ferries.

KEIZERSGRACHT

Along with Prinsengracht and Herengracht, Keizersgracht (➤ 147) is part of the Canal Ring (Grachtengordel).

OUDEIJDS ACHTERBURGWAL AND OUDEZIJDS VOORBURGWAL

A contrast to the peaceful, leafy waterways that characterize Amsterdam, these canals are lined with more garish outlets and bars along parts of their length.

PRINSENGRACHT

The outermost of the three concentric ring canals was named after Prince William of Orange. It was dug in the 17th century to house shopkeepers and craftsmen. A stroll along its houseboat-lined, 3.5km (2-mile) length and into adjacent side-streets, particularly in the northern section bordering the Jordaan (➤ 146–147), takes you past cosy brown cafés, notable restaurants and offbeat shops and boutiques.

REGULIERSGRACHT

Take a trip on this canal at night when the close grouping of seven bridges along its route can be best appreciated.

a walk in the old centre

Flirt with the salacious on a stroll through De Wallen, and find there is more to the oldest part of town than sleaze.

Walk past a canal boat dock and a statue of Queen Wilhelmina, into Lange Brugsteeg and Grimburgwal, to Oudezijds Voorburgwal.

You're on Amsterdam University's downtown campus. On the corner in front of you is a 16th-century red-brick, step-gabled house with a view of three canals. To your left, on Oudezijds Voorburgwal, is the Athenaeum Illustre (➤ 86).

Cross over the canal to Oudezijds Achterburgwal. Directly ahead is Oudemanhuispoort (➤ 103), a covered passage lined with second-hand book stalls. Go through and turn left on Kloveniersburgwal.

Across the water, at No 95, you will see the neoclassical Poppenhuis, built in the 1640s for Joan Poppen.

Continue to Oude Hoogstraat and turn left to visit the courtyard of Oostindisch Huis (➤ 102). Return to Kloveniers-burgwal and turn left.

Across the water, at No 29, is the neoclassical Trippenhuis, built between 1660 and 1664 by Justus Vingboons for the arms merchant Trip brothers – with chimneys shaped like cannon barrels. It is actually two houses, one for each of the brothers, disguised by false middle windows to maintain its symmetry. The building is now home to the Netherlands Academy. You pass tiny Klein-Trippenhuis, built for their coachman, at No 26.

> *Keep going to Nieuwmarkt and De Waag (▶ 113). Take Zeedijk, then turn left on Molensteeg into the heart of the Red Light District (▶ 46–47). Keep going across the two canals until you come to Oude Kerk (▶ 102–103).*

Prostitutes' red-lit windows surround the church.

> *Take Wijde Kerksteeg, then turn left on Warmoesstraat, to the Dam.*

Distance 3km (2 miles)
Time 2 hours
Start point Rokin, at Spui ✚ 17G 🚊 4, 9, 14, 16, 24, 25
End point Dam ✚ 5E 🚊 4, 9, 14, 16, 24, 25
Lunch Café Roux (▶ 60); La Ruche (▶ 120)

a cycle ride

along the Amstel

Cycling is a key ingredient in the Amsterdam experience and on this riverside route you get a breath of fresh country air as a bonus. Pause at the start for a look at the Blauwbrug (Blue Bridge).

Facing south (upriver), cycle along the Amstel's east or right bank (the river should be on your right), across Nieuwe Herengracht and Nieuwe Keizersgracht to the Magere Brug (➤ 133). Cross Nieuwe Prinsengracht to a set of locks beside which stands the Koninklijke Theater Carré (➤ 140). Continue over Sarphatistraat to the Amstel InterContinental hotel (➤ 137).

The city's top hotel, the Amstel is favoured by blue bloods, Hollywood superstars and top musicians.

Dogleg around behind the hotel, back to the river on Weesperzijde, and past De IJsbreker contemporary music centre. Continue to the Berlagebrug, where you cross to the left bank.

The bridge, which has red-and-black painted lampposts, was built in 1932 by Hendrik Petrus Berlage, designer of the Beurs van Berlage (➤ 87), and a forerunner of the Amsterdam School of Architecture.

Continue south, past Martin Luther Kingpark and houseboats moored along Amsteldijk, to Amstelpark (➤ 128), the De Rieker windmill and a statue of the artist Rembrandt.

You are now in open countryside, passing through idyllic riverside scenery on the way to Ouderkerk aan de Amstel. Explore the pretty, historic village.

For the return to Amsterdam, take Ouderkerkerdijk on the right bank of the river.

You pass through several hamlets on this tranquil road.

Keep going to busy Utrechtsebrug. Cross over to Amsteldijk and stay on the left bank all the way back to the Blue Bridge.

Distance 20km (12.5 miles)
Time 4–6 hours
Start/end point Blauwbrug 🕇 19H 🚇 Waterlooplein 🚌 9, 14 🚢 Museum Boat stop 3
Lunch 't Klein Kalfje (€) ✉ Amsteldijk 355
Bicycle rental MacBike ✉ Mr Visserplein 2 ☎ 620 0985

Nightclubs

Akhnaton
World music, salsa, rap and reggae.
✉ Nieuwezijds Kolk 25 ☎ 624 3396 🚌 1, 2, 5, 6, 13, 17

Café West-Pacific
A bar/restaurant where after dinner the tables are pushed away to clear the floor and it becomes a nightclub. This is a trendy venue and you might have to pay membership.
✉ Harlemmerweg 6–10, Westerpark ☎ 597 4458 🚌 10

Club Arena
See page 137.

Escape
The biggest disco in town; you'll need to be smartly dressed to get in and might face a wait. The most popular night is Saturday.
✉ Rembrandtplein 11 ☎ 622 1111 🚌 4, 9, 14

Exit
One of the most widely known gay clubs in the city. There are three floors and the dance area is overlooked by a balcony. The music is contemporary dance and the light show high tech.
✉ Reguliersdwarsstraat 42 ☎ 625 8788 🚌 1, 2, 4, 5, 9, 14, 16, 20

Flexbar
Open Fridays and Saturdays, occasionally Thursdays and Sundays, but always till the early hours, the Flexbar dishes up hip-hop and electro and has two dance spaces on two floors. Very popular.
✉ Pazzanistraat 1 ☎ 486 2123; www.flexbar.nl 🚌 2, 5

Jimmy Woo
Hot new club that mixes ancient Chinese with hyper-modern design. Where the in people like to be seen.
✉ Korte Leidsedwarsstraat 18 ☎ 626 3150 🚌 1, 2, 5

Odeon

Dance club in a 17th-century canal house that retains its character while offering a contemporary arena. The balcony bar overlooks the dance floor.

✉ Singel 460 ☎ 624 9711 🚊 1, 2, 5

Paradiso

Rock, reggae and pop, live and disco, in a former church. Mainly a live music venue, but sometimes has visiting and international DJs at weekends.

✉ Weteringschans 6–8 ☎ 626 4521 🚊 1, 2, 5, 6, 7, 10

Studio 80

Old radio studio turned into a dance venue for disco, hip-hop, techno and every other modern style, with gay-friendly Wednesdays.

✉ Rembrandtplein 17 ☎ 521 8333; www.studio-80.nl 🚊 4, 9, 14, 16, 24, 25

Places to stay

This is a selection of the best hotels from all price categories.

Agora (€€)
One of the best budget hotels, near Bloemenmarkt. Some rooms have views of the Amstel and some overlook a garden.
✉ Singel 462 ☎ 627 2200; www.hotelagora.nl 🚌 4, 9, 14, 16, 24, 25

Ambassade (€€)
The 59 rooms are shared across 10 canal houses. Each room is individual but all are furnished in Louis XV or XVI style.
✉ Herengracht 341 ☎ 555 0222; www.ambassade-hotel.nl 🚌 1, 2, 5

Amstel InterContinental (€€€)
See page 137.

Amsterdam Weichmann (€)
Another good budget option – three old charming canal houses on the Jordaan.
✉ Prinsengracht 328–332 ☎ 626 3321; www.hotelwiechmann.nl 🚌 1, 2, 5

Canal House (€€)

Two canal houses merged to form a hotel. Its star attraction is the breakfast room which reflects the houses' 17th-century heyday.

✉ Keizersgracht 148 ☎ 622 5182; www.canalhouse.nl 🚌 6, 13, 14, 17

The Dylan (€€€)

This is a compact boutique hotel with superb style, courtesy of interior designer/hotelier Anoushka Hempel. Each of the 41 rooms is colour-themed with oriental touches.

✉ Keizersgracht 384 ☎ 530 2010; www.dylanamsterdam.com
🚌 1, 2, 5

Estheréa (€€€)

A 71-room canalside hotel in the centre of Amsterdam. If you can, opt for a room that overlooks the canal.

✉ Singel 303–309 ☎ 624 5146; www.estherea.nl 🚌 1, 2, 5

The Lloyd (€€€)

Trendy hotel with individually designed cool and contemporary rooms.

✉ Oostelijke Handelskade 34 ☎ 561 3636; www.lloydhotel.com
🚌 IJtram

Seven Bridges (€€)

See page 137.

Sofitel The Grand Amsterdam (€€€)

The bedrooms reflect the age and splendour of the building with high ceilings and large windows that overlook courtyards or canals.

✉ Oudezijds Voorburgwal 197 ☎ 555 3111; www.thegrand.nl
🚇 Nieuwmarkt

Shopping

De Bijenkorf

Flagship, up-market department store with a staggering array of goods ranging from household items to own-label and designer clothes. At Christmas the store is beautifully decorated and attracts lots of visitors.

✉ Dam 1 ☎ 552 1700 🚊 4, 9, 14, 16, 24, 25

Bonebakker

Royal jewellers with an enticing, if pricey, display of glittering jewellery and gold and silverware. Come just to window-shop if you don't want to purchase the wonders on offer.

✉ Rokin 88–90 ☎ 623 2294 🚊 4, 9, 14, 16, 24, 25

Frozen Fountain

A shop that sells furniture, lighting and accessories, including classic labels, but also a showcase for up-and-coming interior designers. Exhibitions are also held here. A good place to find a gift.

✉ Prinsengracht 645 ☎ 622 9375 🚊 1, 2, 5

Galleria Arte de Rinascimento

A range of Delftware, from the expensive DePorcelyne Fles to affordable souvenirs and Christmas trinkets.

✉ Prinsengracht 170 ☎ 622 7509 🚊 6, 13, 14, 17

Gassan Diamonds

Not just a shop, but a tour of the factory too, ending up at the shop where you can buy diamonds or diamond jewellery.

✉ Wagenstraat 13–17 ☎ 622 5333 🚊 4, 9, 14

Geels en Co

A respected, and the oldest, coffee roasting and tea merchant in Amsterdam. Helpful staff sell chocolate and coffee pots

as well as numerous teas and coffees.
Upstairs there is a small museum.
✉ Warmoesstraat 67 ☎ 624 0683 🚊 4, 9, 14, 16,
24, 25

Holland Gallery de Munt

A treasure trove of ceramics, glassware, dolls.
Also antique Delftware and traditional tiles.
✉ Muntplein 12 ☎ 623 2271 🚊 4, 9, 14, 16, 24, 25

Jordino

A treat for those with a sweet tooth. This shop
sells chocolate and marzipan delights, along
with ice cream made on the premises.
✉ Harlemmerdijk 25a ☎ 420 3225 🚊 1, 2, 5, 6,
13, 17

Metz & Co

See page 154.

Oilily

The children's branch of a Dutch clothing
company that is now international. Children
will love the cheerful and bright designs and
their mothers will be attracted to the fun and
colourful adult clothing.
✉ Singel 457 ☎ 422 8713 🚊 1, 4, 9, 14, 16, 24, 25

Exploring

Any one of the elements that meld to form Amsterdam's special character would be enough to create a memorable setting. Its thousands of magnificent 17th-century buildings, strung along a web of canals crossed by more than a thousand bridges; its situation below sea-level in a place where, by rights, cold North Sea waves should flow back and forth; the centuries-long tradition of tolerance that made the city a magnet for oppressed minorities long before such a stance became fashionable, or even imaginable, elsewhere; the refusal to settle for what outsiders consider right and proper, but instead to search for their own solutions to all kinds of social challenges, from prostitution, to drug use and abuse; and how to live harmoniously in a melting-pot society. The city's often eccentric lifestyle has a downside, and not everybody takes to its free and easy ways. One thing is sure, though: you'll never be bored.

Central Amsterdam

The medieval core of the city is punctuated by canals and includes areas of calm and tranquillity alongside the brash Red Light District and tourist attractions. Here, too, are some wonderful cafés and restaurants.

The main square is Dam, which is within easy walking distance of the major sights. You might find better shopping elsewhere in the city, but there are some notable shops here. The district's main attractions include Amsterdams Historisch Museum and Begijnhof and, of course, the Red Light District.

ALLARD PIERSON MUSEUM

Amsterdam University houses its archaeological collection in a neoclassical former bank. There are few outstanding objects, but rather bits and pieces from here and there – coins, funerary monuments, mummies, glassware, jewellery, marble, pottery, sculpture and everyday objects. Pharaonic Egypt, Minoan Crete, ancient Greece, Rome and Etruria are reasonably well represented, and there are some good models of pyramids and chariots. Temporary exhibitions are generally more interesting.

➕ 18G ✉ Oude Turfmarkt 127 ☎ 525 2556 🕐 Tue–Fri 10–5, Sat–Sun and public hols 1–5. Closed 1 Jan, Easter Sun, 30 Apr, 5 May, Whit Sunday, 25 Dec ✋ Moderate 🚌 4, 9, 14, 16, 24, 25

AMSTERDAMS HISTORISCH MUSEUM

Best places to see, ➤ 36–37.

ATHENAEUM ILLUSTRE

A Renaissance gateway from 1571 marks the entrance to Amsterdam's first university. Founded in 1631, it took over the 15th-century Gothic Agnietenkapel (St Agnes Chapel) and Franciscan convent, which was used as an arsenal by the Dutch navy after the 1578 religious *Alteratie* (Alteration). It now houses the Universiteitsmuseum (University Museum), embracing the university's history, professors and students.

➕ 6F ✉ Oudezijds Voorburgwal 231 ☎ 525 3339 🕐 Mon–Fri 9–5, Sun (late Jun to mid-Nov) 2–5. Closed public hols ✋ Free (except special exhibitions) 🚌 4, 9, 14, 16, 24, 25

BEGIJNHOF

Best places to see, ➤ 40–41.

BEURS VAN BERLAGE

Hendrik Petrus Berlage's 1903, red-brick Beurs (Stock Exchange) is an early work of the Amsterdam School, whose members made a dramatic break with 19th-century architecture. No longer the stock exchange, it hosts concerts and exhibitions with displays about the Stock Exchange's history and temporary exhibitions about varying themes. The interior has interesting glass and wrought-iron decoration and murals. Among exterior sculptures, a relief of two fishermen and a sick dog in a boat illustrates a legend of the city's foundation. Climb the clock tower for a view of the old centre. Trees and 19th-century wrought-iron street lamps dot neighbouring Beursplein.

✚ 6E ✉ Damrak 243 ☎ 530 4141 ⊕ Exhibitions: daily 10–10 ✋ Free 🍴 Café Rainieri (€) 🚊 4, 9, 14, 16, 24, 25

BLOEMENMARKT

Like an Impressionist artist's palette fallen from the sky, the Singel Flower Market, Amsterdam's only remaining floating market (though it no longer floats, exactly), is a riot of colour. A floating market was established here in the 17th century; now a row of 15 shops partially installed on permanently moored barges sell freshly cut flowers as fast as the staff can wrap them, along with plants, packets of tulip bulbs with phytosanitary certificates that permit their import into many countries, and all kinds of green-fingered accessories. Buying flowers along the fragrantly scented canalside is an Amsterdam ritual.

🚊 17H ✉ Singel (between Muntplein and Koningsplein) 🕐 Mon–Fri 9–6, Sat 9–5 ✋ Free 🚋 1, 2, 4, 5, 9, 14, 16, 24, 25 🚤 Museum Boat stop 4

CENTRAAL STATION

Amsterdam's main railway station is a bustling hub that captures the city's energy, bundles it up and sends it off in all directions. Eleven of 16 tram lines converge here, along with four metro lines, passenger ferries, any number of buses, canal buses, taxis, water-taxis and tour boats (including the Museumboat and the Canal Bus). There are two VVV (Vereniging voor Vreemdelingen Verkeer) city tourist offices, one inside on platform two, the other outside on Stationsplein; a Grenswisselkantoor (GWK) exchange office; cafés; shops; buskers; barrel-organs; a million bicycles, commuters, tourists, backpackers, pickpockets and junkies.

Petrus Josephus Hubertus Cuypers designed this work of architectural note, which opened in 1889 on three artificial islands in the IJ channel. Cuypers, who also designed the Rijksmuseum (➤ 48–49), repeated his particular mix of Dutch Renaissance elements with his own neo-Gothic inclinations, to produce a twin-towered temple of transport that many Amsterdammers, at the time, disliked.

🚊 7D ✉ Stationsplein 🍴 1e Klas (€–€€), Smits Koffiehuis (€) 🚋 1, 2, 4, 5, 6, 9, 13, 16, 17, 24, 25 🚤 Museum Boat stop 1

DAM

Foreigners say 'Dam Square', but to Amsterdammers it's 'the Dam', though it is evidently a square and not a dam. The original dam, built in the early-13th century, protected what was then a fishing village. As Amsterdam expanded, flood defences were built farther away and the Dam developed into the political, commercial, monumental and ceremonial heart of the city, containing the Royal Palace (➤ 42–43), Nieuwe Kerk (➤ 101) and Nationaal Monument (➤ 99). It frequently hosts fairs, concerts and other events.

➕ 5E 🚌 1, 2, 4, 6, 5, 9, 13, 14, 16, 17, 24, 25

EROTISCH MUSEUM

'The Art of Erotics' is how the owners subtitle their establishment. Prints and drawings, including some by John Lennon, and photographs aim to uncover the artistic side of eroticism and sado-masochism. Attractions include a maquette (scale model) of a Red Light District scene and an adult cartoon version of *Snow White and the Seven Dwarfs*.

➕ 7E ✉ Oudezijds Achterburgwal 54 ☎ 624 7303 🕐 Mon–Thu, Sun 11am–1am; Fri–Sat 11am–2am ✋ Moderate 🚌 4, 9, 14, 16, 24, 25

HASH MARIHUANA HEMP MUSEUM

An 'educational' tour informs you of the good things that ostensibly flow from smoking and otherwise assimilating hemp's multifarious, stimulating by-products. You will see displays on historical, medicinal, religious, recreational and practical uses of hashish and marijuana.

🕇 6E ✉ Oudezijds Achterburgwal 130 ☎ 623 5961 🕓 Daily 10–10 🖐 Moderate 🚊 4, 9, 14, 16, 24, 25

HERENGRACHT

Best places to see, ➤ 70–71.

HET IJ

The IJ (pronounced like 'eye' in English), an inlet of the IJsselmeer lake, was once the city's harbour. In the 17th century, warehouses filled with exotic products brought from all over the world lined the waterfront. Although large cargo ships now use newer facilities west of the city, beside the North Sea Canal, the IJ remains busy with canal barges, pleasure craft, tour boats and an occasional warship and cruise liner. Free passenger-and-bicycle ferries shuttle back and forth across the channel between the rear of Centraal Station and Amsterdam-Noord, affording a fine view of the harbour during their brief crossings. On Sundays and public holidays (excluding Koninginnedag, 30 April) from Easter until mid-October, a Historic Ferry tour leaves

from the dock behind Centraal Station for cruises around the old harbour installations in the eastern IJ.

For an insight into the IJ's colourful maritime past, visit the Nederlands Scheepvaartmuseum (➤ 134) and the redeveloped Western and Eastern Islands, on either side of Centraal Station.

🚇 7C 🚊 Centraal Station 🚌 1, 2, 4, 5, 6, 9, 13, 16, 17, 24, 25 🚢 Museum Boat stop 1 ❓ Historic Ferry cruises leave at 12, 2 and 4; duration two hours

JODENHOEK

Jewish refugees escaping persecution in Europe began arriving in Amsterdam in the 16th century, settling on cheap, marshy land between Nieuwmarkt and the Amstel, around what is now Waterlooplein and Jodenbreestraat. Little remains of the once thriving Jewish Quarter, which, until World War II, never descended to the status of a ghetto. Of the city's 60,000-strong pre-war Jewish population, only about 6,000 survived the Holocaust. During the 1944–45 Hunger Winter, Amsterdammers stripped wood from the quarter's empty buildings to burn as fuel, and many unsafe houses were demolished after the war, with more falling victim to redevelopment. Remnants and echoes include the Joods Historisch Museum (➤ opposite), the Hollandsche Schouwburg (➤ 131), the 1675 Portugees-Israëlietische Synagoge (➤ 104), Waterlooplein Flea Market (➤ 114), and a Waterlooplein monument to Jewish Resistance fighters.

✚ 19G 🚇 Waterlooplein, Nieuwmarkt 🚌 9, 14 ⛴ Museum Boat stop 3

JOODS HISTORISCH MUSEUM

The remarkable Jewish Historical Museum, occupying four former synagogues in the heart of the Jewish Quarter (see opposite), records four centuries of Jewish history, identity, religion and culture in the Netherlands. Glassed-in walkways connect the Ashkenazi Synagogue (1670) to the Obbene (1686), Dritt (1700) and New (1752) synagogues. Located here since 1987, the museum puts on temporary exhibitions about international Jewish themes in addition to displaying its permanent collection, which includes historical paintings, decorations, religious and ceremonial objects, clothing, a section on the Holocaust and contemporary Jewish art.

In the square behind the museum is a sculpture called *The Dockworker*, commemorating the February 1941 general strike, led by the city's dockworkers, against Nazi deportation of the Jewish population.

✚ 20G ✉ Nieuwe Amstelstraat 1 ☎ 531 0310 🕐 Daily 11–5 (Thu till 9pm). Closed Yom Kippur ✋ Expensive 🍴 Kosher café (€) 🚇 Waterlooplein 🚌 9, 14 ⛴ Museum Boat stop 3

KONINKLIJK PALEIS

Best places to see, ➤ 42–43.

MADAME TUSSAUD

More than a gallery of
waxen Dutch stares, this
waxworks uses audio-
animatronics, climate-
control, smell generators
and other special effects to
bring to life Holland from
the Golden Age onwards.
You will see Rembrandt, Vermeer, Jan Steen and others at work.
Kings, princes, merchants and peasants put in an appearance.
Walk-through scenes include an Amsterdam canalside, a brown
café and ice-skating, and there are such famous Dutch characters
as Erasmus, Mata Hari and Johann Cruyff, as well as international
greats, including Churchill, Einstein and Gandhi.

✚ 5E ✉ Dam 20 ☎ 523 0623 🕔 Daily 10–5:30 (occasionally till 9pm).
Closed 30 Apr 🖐 Very expensive 🚊 4, 9, 14, 16, 24, 25

MUNTTOREN

The Mint Tower's base is all that remains of the 1490 Reguliers
Gate in the demolished city wall. It got its present name in
1672–73, during the war with England and France, when coins
were minted here. In 1620, Hendrick de Keyser, who had already
topped the Montelbaanstoren, added an ornate, lead-covered
spire. A tinkling carillon breaks every hour into classical, folk or pop
music, and on Friday from noon until 1pm the bells play a mini-
concert. The tower is closed to the public except for a ground-floor
shop selling blue porcelain.

Look for a carving on the attached building, which was once a
guardhouse and is now a souvenir shop, depicting an alternative
tale of Amsterdam's foundation: the image of two men and a
seasick dog in a boat.

✚ 18G ✉ Muntplein 🚊 4, 9, 14, 16, 24, 25

MUSEUM AMSTELKRING

You get two museums in one here. First is the canal house, built between 1661 and 1663 by merchant Jan Hartman, who sold stockings in a ground-floor shop. Its 17th-century oak furniture, paintings and decoration give a superb idea of period life. Hartman was Catholic and, as a 1578 law prohibited Catholic services, he turned the attics of this and two adjacent houses he also owned into a *schuilkerk*, a clandestine church. Of many such churches, only this one has been completely preserved. Historians of the Amstelkring (Amstel Circle) saved it from demolition in 1888 and named it Ons' Lieve Heer op Solder (Our Lord in the Attic). You climb a narrow stairway to the third-floor church, remodelled in baroque style in 1739 and with many of its original religious objects, including Jacob de Wit's painting *The Baptism of Christ* (1736). An occasional service is still held, as are recitals.

✚ 6D ✉ Oudezijds Voorburgwal 40 ☎ 624 6604 🕐 Mon–Sat 10–5, Sun and public hols 1–5. Closed 1 Jan, 30 Apr 🖐 Moderate 🚇 Centraal Station 🚌 1, 2, 4, 5, 6, 9, 13, 14, 16, 17, 24, 25 ⛴ Museum Boat stop 1

MUSEUM HET REMBRANDTHUIS

The great Dutch artist Rembrandt van Rijn (1606–69) owned this house (built in 1606) from 1639, when his work was in constant demand, until he was forced to sell in 1658 because of bankruptcy. Restoration work, completed in 2001, has returned the house to

the way it looked when Rembrandt lived and worked in it. The combined living room and bedroom, and Rembrandt's studio, are highlights of the tour. His wife, Saskia van Uylenburgh, died here in 1642, aged 30, shortly after their son Titus was born in the house. You can also see paintings by his teacher, Pieter Lastman, and some of his students. Around 250 of Rembrandt's 300 surviving engravings and drawings are on display in the exhibition wing (opened in 1998) next door, including portraits, self-portraits and landscapes.

✚ 7F ✉ Jodenbreestraat 4–6 ☎ 520 0400 🕐 Daily 10–5. Closed 1 Jan
✋ Expensive 🚇 Waterlooplein 🚊 9, 14 🚤 Museum Boat stop 3

MUSEUM WILLET-HOLTHUYSEN

Another patrician canal house-turned-museum, this one was built in 1687 for a member of the city council, Jacob Hop. In 1855 Pieter Gerard Holthuysen, a glass merchant, bought it and, in due course, his daughter Sandrina and her husband, Abraham Willett, inherited the house. The couple built up a valuable collection of glass, silver, porcelain and paintings and in 1895 turned over the lot, house included, to an unenthusiastic city council for use as a museum. Following renovation the museum has been attracting an

increasing number of visitors to its 18th-century basement kitchen, Victorian bedrooms, the Blue Room, with its painted ceiling – *Dawn Chasing Away Night*, by Jacob de Wit (1744) – and dining salon with places set for a banquet.

✚ 19H ✉ Herengracht 605 ☎ 523 1822 🕐 Mon–Fri 10–5, Sat–Sun 11–5. Closed 1 Jan, 30 April, 25 Dec ✋ Moderate 🚌 4, 9, 14 🚢 Museum Boat stop 3

NATIONAAL MONUMENT

The National Monument, an obelisk with symbolic sculptures, was erected in 1956 to commemorate the victims of Holland's occupation by Nazi Germany during World War II. Over the years it has become a popular meeting place.

✚ 5E ✉ Dam 🚌 4, 9, 14, 16, 24, 25

NEMO

Technology and science are the related themes at this interactive museum housed in a spectacular, modern building from 1997 by Italian architect Renzo Piano in Amsterdam harbour. NEMO brings you face to face with the latest developments through such hands-on virtual activities as steering a supertanker, trading shares, generating power and performing surgery. You can conduct scientific experiments in a laboratory, do basic research on natural phenomena, play computer games, watch tech-orientated demonstrations, movies and theatre performances, listen to debates, surf the web and tour temporary exhibitions. The rooftop terrace has become a popular spot for soaking up sun and watching the sunset.

www.e-nemo.nl

🚇 9E ✉ Oosterdok 2 ☎ 531 3233 🕐 Tue–Sun 10–5 (also Mon Jun–Aug and school holidays). Closed 1 Jan, 30 Apr, 25 Dec 🖐 Expensive 🍴 Café with waterside terrace (€); cafeteria with rooftop terrace (€–€€) 🚌 Bus 22, 32 ⛴ Museum Boat stop 2

NIEUWE KERK

The New Church has been Holland's coronation church since 1815, but is now mostly used for art exhibitions and cultural events. It dates from 1408, though an original Gothic structure was destroyed by fire in 1521. Calvinists stripped out the Catholic ornamentation after their 1578 takeover.

Where the high altar once stood is an elaborate marble memorial to Admiral Michiel de Ruyter (1607–76), who in 1667 singed the King of England's beard by sailing up the Medway and destroying an English fleet. Sculpted by Rombout Verhulst, it depicts the hero lying on a cannon, surrounded by sea creatures. Poets Pieter Cornelisz Hooft (1581–1647) and Joost van den Vondel (1587–1679) are buried in the church in unmarked graves.

✚ 5E ✉ Dam ☎ 638 6909 ⏰ Daily 10–6 (Thu till 10 during exhibitions) ♿ Free (special exhibitions range from moderate to very expensive) 🍴 Nieuwe Café (€€) 🚋 1, 2, 4, 5, 6, 9, 13, 14, 16, 17, 24, 25

NIEUWMARKT

A seedy area well into the 1980s, where heroin addicts and ne'er-do-wells hung out, the market square's character was appropriate, as this was once the site of public executions, and bits and pieces of dismembered criminals were hung up on De Waag (➤ 113) as a warning to others. Having been cleaned up, it is becoming a popular, alternative nightlife zone. At the heart of the city's Chinatown, it has many authentic, inexpensive Chinese eateries, as well as good traditional Dutch cafés with pavement terraces. Just off the square, on Zeedijk, is the new Buddist Fo Guang Shan He Hua Temple, a remarkable sight on this bustling street.

✚ 7E 🍴 Many cafés (€) and restaurants (€–€€) Ⓜ Nieuwmarkt

OOSTINDISCH HUIS

This is the former headquarters of the once-powerful Veerenigde Oostindische Compagnie (United East India Company), which was founded in 1602. Its occupants once sent expeditions to the Orient to bring back silks, spices and other riches that fuelled Amsterdam's Golden Age. They controlled their own army and had authority to declare war and make treaties. Hendrick de Keyser's red brick and yellow sandstone building, dating from 1605 to 1606, now belongs to Amsterdam University; you can stroll into its courtyard, and by pretending to be a student can peruse the interior.

✚ 6F ✉ Oude Hoogstraat 24 🚋 4, 9, 14, 16, 24, 25

OUDE KERK

The Gothic Old Church, begun in 1334, stands in the heart of the Red Light District, surrounded by former almshouses. In summer you can climb the spire, built by Joost Bilhamer in 1555, and on Saturday between 4 and 5pm the carillon bursts into tune. Not

much Catholic ornamentation survived the Calvinist takeover, but in the Mariakapel you can see three superb stained-glass windows. Composer Jan Sweelinck (1562–1621) is buried in the church where he was organist for 45 years, as are Rembrandt's wife Saskia, a squadron of 17th-century admirals and poet Maria Tesselschade, who died in 1649.

🔚 6E ✉ Oudekerksplein 23 ☎ 625 8284 ⏰ Church: Mon–Sat 11–5, Sun 1–5. Tower: Jun–Sep Wed–Sun 2–4; Sep–Apr Sun–Fri 1–5, Sat 11–5. Closed 1 Jan, 30 Apr 🖐 Moderate 🚇 Nieuwmarkt 🚌 4, 9, 14, 16, 24, 25

OUDEMANHUISPOORT

Once the entrance to a hospice for elderly men, this long covered passage dating from 1601 beside Amsterdam University now houses antiquarian and second-hand book stalls that spread their wares on tables lining the arcade. Midway along, on either side, are doors that open onto Amsterdam University's law department buildings; the doors on the left lead first to a courtyard garden with a sculpted head of Minerva in the middle.

🔚 6F ⏰ Mon–Sat 10–4 🚌 4, 9, 14, 16, 24, 25

PORTUGEES-ISRAËLIETISCHE SYNAGOGE

Sephardic Jews fleeing persecution in Spain and Portugal began to settle in Amsterdam during the 1580s, bringing a touch of colour to the sober, Calvinist city. As a sign of their prosperity in a relatively tolerant environment, they pooled their wealth to build the lavish Portuguese-Israelite Synagogue (1671–75), designed by Elias Bouman. Wooden barrel vaults supported on Ionic columns form the interior, which is decorated with low-hanging brass chandeliers.

✚ 20G ✉ Mr Visserplein 1 ☎ 624 5351 🕐 Apr–Oct Sun–Fri 10–4; Nov–Mar Sun–Thu 10–4, Fri 10–2. Closed Sat and Jewish hols (except for services) ♿ Moderate 🚇 Waterlooplein 🚌 9, 14 🚢 Museum Boat stop 3

PRINSENHOF

The Prince's House was the St Cecilia Convent until the 1578 Protestant Alteration, when the city commandeered it as a lodging house. In 1647, the Admiralty moved in, and when, in 1808, Louis Napoleon turfed the city councillors out of their town hall on the Dam, they moved here. Since the council left in 1986, the Prinsenhof has become the Grand Hotel, a predominantly 1920s Amsterdam School structure. In its Café Roux (➤ 60), you can see a 1949 mural, *Inquisitive Children*, by CoBrA artist Karel Appel.

✚ 6F ✉ Oudezijds Voorburgwal 197 ☎ 555 3111 🍴 Café Roux (€€) 🚌 4, 9, 14, 16, 24, 25

RED LIGHT DISTRICT

Best places to see, ➤ 46–47.

REMBRANDTPLEIN

Brash and bustling Rembrandtplein jumps at night with music from the mostly unmemorable cafés that surround it. A bronze statue of Rembrandt (1852) by Louis Royer, in the middle of the square, doesn't look much like the down-at-heel self-portraits the artist typically painted. While you're here, visit the magnificent, art deco Tuschinski Cinema (1921) at adjacent Reguliersbreestraat 26 – you can wander around the lobby, and in July and August join guided tours.

✚ 18H 🍴 Café Schiller (€–€€); Grand Café l'Opera (€–€€); Royal Café de Kroon (€–€€) 🚊 4, 9, 14, 16, 24, 25 ❓ Guided tours Sun and Mon at 10:30

SCHEEPVAARTHUIS

Maritime House, noted for its curving lines and marine motifs, is a work of the Amsterdam School, which flowered briefly early in the 20th century. Designed by Michel de Klerk, Pieter Kramer and Johan van der May between 1912 and 1913 for a consortium of local shipping companies, it now houses the city's municipal transport authority, the GVB. It is ornamented with portrait busts of famous captains, navigators and cartographers. Nearby, at Prins Hendrikkade 131, is a house that once belonged to the 17th-century admiral, Michiel de Ruyter.

✚ 7E ✉ Prins Hendrikkade 108–114 🕐 Mon–Fri 9–4:30 🚇 Centraal Station 🚌 Bus 22, 32, 33, 34, 35, 39

SCHREIERSTOREN

The Weeping Tower began life around 1480 as a heavily fortified strong point in the city wall overlooking the harbour. Its somewhat fanciful name comes from the tears sailors' wives and sweethearts ostensibly shed from its ramparts as ships sailed away on long and often fatal voyages to the East and West Indies. A plaque on the wall shows such an apparently distraught woman watching a ship depart. Other plaques on the tower record Henry Hudson's 1609 voyage to what was to be known as New York and the Hudson River, and Cornelis Houtman's 1595 voyage to Indonesia; both expeditions left from the harbour here.

🚌 7D ✉ Prins Hendrikkade 94–95 🍴 VOC Café (€) 🚊 Centraal Station
🚊 1, 2, 4, 5, 9, 13, 16, 17, 24, 25; bus 22, 32 ⛴ Museum Boat stop 1

SCHUTTERSGALERIJ

The Civic Guards Gallery, belonging to the Amsterdams Historisch Museum (➤ 36–37), displays 15 vast 16th- and 17th-century group portraits of the city's Civic Guards, local militia companies, such as the detail shown opposite, hung in a covered passageway. One of the canvases on display is *The Company of Captain Joan Huydecoper, 1648*, painted by Rembrandt's student Govert Flinck.

🚌 5F ✉ Kalverstraat 92, Nieuwezijds Voorburgwal 359, Sint-Luciënsteeg 27
☎ 523 1822 🕐 Mon–Fri 10–5, Sat–Sun and public hols 11–5 ✋ Free 🚊 1,
2, 4, 5, 9, 14, 16, 24, 25 ⛴ Museum Boat stop 4

SEXMUSEUM AMSTERDAM

Once you get past the 'cultural' stuff, a false marble entrance in the shape of a classical pediment, you're into the Sex Museum's serious business, which ranges from naughty to downright dirty. Mannequins bring you close to the 'action'. Other exhibits include toys, trinkets, specialized clothing and appliances.

🚌 6D ✉ Damrak 18 ☎ 622 8376 🕐 Daily 10am–11pm ✋ Inexpensive
🚊 Centraal Station 🚊 1, 2, 4, 5, 6, 9, 13, 16, 17, 24, 25 ⛴ Museum Boat
stop 1 ❓ No admission to under-16s

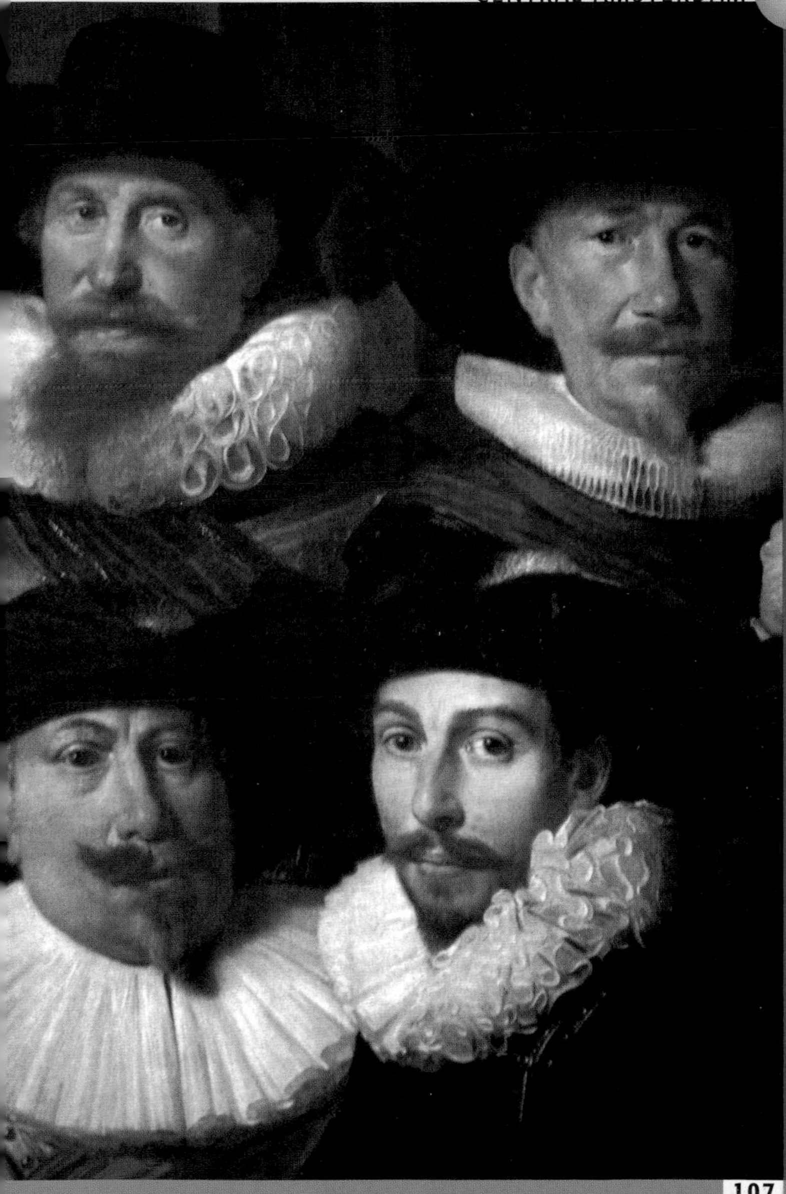

SINGEL

Before the city embarked on its Golden Age expansion, this canal formed a moat outside the walls. By the early 17th century it was a residential zone and the earliest ring canal. There are few major monuments on its 1.7km (1-mile) course through the city between Prins Hendrikkade, near Centraal Station, and the Munttoren (► 96), beside the Flower Market (► 88–89), yet a stroll along its length is full of minor interest. The Nieuwe Haarlemmersluis beside Brouwersgracht, an outlet from the canals, plays an important part in the 1.5-hour thorough cleansing the system gets every night, when fresh water is pumped through to flush the canals out. Near here, moored beside Singel 40, is the *Poezenboot*, a refuge for dozens of stray cats. The Torensluis at Oude Leliestraat is the city's widest bridge.

Among Singel's most interesting churches is the Ronde Lutherse Koepelkerk (Round Domed Lutheran Church), built between 1668 and 1671 by Adriaen Dortsman for the city's Lutheran community and now used by the Renaissance Amsterdam Hotel as a conference centre.

🕂 4F 🍴 Cafés and restaurants (€–€€€) 🚊 1, 2, 4, 5, 6, 9, 13, 14, 16, 17, 24, 25 ⛴ Museum Boat stop 1, 4

SINGEL 7

Canal boat tour guides point out the façade of this 16th-century house as the city's narrowest, at 1m (3ft) wide – an important consideration in times past, as the wider the canal frontage, the more a building cost. Singel 7 cleverly uses a narrow frontage then widens to a more usual size behind the façade.

🕂 5D 🚊 1, 2, 5, 6, 13, 17

SINT-NICOLAASKERK

With its twin towers and tall, domed cupola, the city's main Catholic church (1888), dedicated to St Nicholas, is a highly visible landmark facing Centraal Station. The church's richly decorated interior is almost neobaroque, its square pillars topped with Corinthian capitals. The marble high altar is flanked by bronze reliefs recalling the 1345 Miracle of Amsterdam: on the right Emperor Maximilian gives Amsterdam the imperial crown after being cured of illness following a visit to the Sacrament Chapel; on the left is a depiction of the Miracle Procession. In addition to being the patron saint of Amsterdam and sailors, St Nicholas is Sinterklaas, Holland's traditional version of Santa Claus, who on the night of 5 December – *Sinterklaasavond*, or *Pakjesavond* – delivers presents to sleeping children.

✠ 7D ✉ Prins Hendrikkade 73 ☎ 684 4803 🕐 Tue–Fri 11–4, Sat, Mon 12–3; Sun services ✋ Free 🚊 Centraal Station 🚌 1, 2, 4, 5, 6, 9, 13, 16, 17, 24, 25 🚤 Museum Boat stop 1

STEDELIJK MUSEUM CS

The modern art Municipal Museum's building at Museumplein, which opened in 1895, and its new wing from 1954 are both closed until some time late in 2009 for major renovation. In the meantime, the museum has taken up temporary quarters in the TPG Gebouw Building close to Centraal Station.

Things change fast at the Stedelijk and you never know what will be on view. The permanent collection includes De Stijl works by Piet Mondrian, CoBrA by Karel Appel and abstract expressionism by Willem de Kooning. Among many other artists represented are Calder, Cézanne, Chagall, Manet, Monet, Oldenburg, Picasso, Renoir, Rosenquist, Van Gogh and Warhol, and there's also a large collection of abstract paintings by Russian artist Kasimir Malevich. There is strong public demand to view the Stedelijk's works from around 1900 until the 1970s, while the healthy private-gallery scene in the city allows the very latest art to be viewed elsewhere.

🚋 8D ✉ TPG Gebouw (Building), Oosterdokskade 3–5 ☎ 573 2911
🕐 Daily 10–6. Closed 1 Jan, 30 Apr, 25 Dec ✋ Expensive
🚉 Centraal Station 🚌 1, 2, 4, 5, 6, 13, 16, 17, 24 ⛴ Museum Boat stop 2

TORENSLUIS

The widest bridge in the old town stands on the site of a 17th-century sluice gate flanked by twin towers that were demolished in 1829. Its foundations were used for what must have been a particularly damp and gloomy prison. Today, outdoor terraces encroach onto the bridge from nearby cafés. The bronze statue is of Multatuli (Eduard Douwes Dekker), a 19th-century author.

✚ 5E ✉ Singel (at Oude Leliestraat)
🚌 1, 2, 5, 6, 13, 17

WAAG

Built in 1488, the moated and fortified Sint-Antoniespoort gateway in the city walls was converted into a weigh-house and guild headquarters in 1617. Rembrandt's *The Anatomy Lesson of Dr Tulp* (1632), depicting a dissection by Surgeon's Guild members, was painted here in the preserved upper floor Theatrum Anatomicum. With the city walls long vanished and the moat filled in to form Nieuwmarkt, the Waag now houses a multi-media foundation, and has a fine café-restaurant, In de Waag, on the ground floor.

✚ 7E ✉ Nieuwmarkt ☎ Café: 422 7772
🕐 Rarely open to the public (except café-restaurant) ✋ Free (charge for some exhibitions) 🍴 Café-restaurant (➤ 121)
🚇 Nieuwmarkt 🚌 4, 9, 14, 16, 24, 25

WATERLOOPLEIN

Once the heart of Amsterdam's Jewish Quarter, the
square and its surroundings have been brutalized by
'development' projects since the end of the war,
when it lay in ruins. A spark of the old life survives in
the Waterlooplein Vlooienmarkt (flea market), which
may have lost the colour of its Jewish heyday, but retains the
charm intrinsic to a market that retails everything from valuable
antiques to trash. The 1980s, postmodern Stadhuis (Town Hall) and
Muziektheater (Opera), occupy the centre of the square. Between
the two is the Normaal Amsterdams Peil (Amsterdam Ordnance
Datum), a bronze plaque that sets Europe's altitude standard; one
of the three water-filled glass columns beside it shows the high-
water mark of the 1953 Zeeland floods.

✚ 19G ✉ Waterlooplein 🕓 Market: Mon–Fri 9–5, Sat 8:30–5:30
🍴 Grand Café Dantzig (€€) 🚇 Waterlooplein 🚌 9, 14 🚢 Museum Boat
stop 3

ZUIDERKERK

Built by Hendrick de Keyser between 1603 and 1614, the city's
first, new, post-Reformation Protestant church has not been used
for religious purposes since 1929. It now houses the municipal
town planning information centre and an exhibition on recent and
proposed urban development. At certain times you can climb the
Italianate church's ornate bell tower, the Zuidertoren, for a
magnificent view over the Nieuwmarkt and Waterlooplein districts.
The churchyard, where Rembrandt's first three children were
buried, has been paved over and surrounded by modern
apartments, but De Keyser's Renaissance gateway, 'decorated'
with carved skulls, still stands beside Sint-Antoniesbreestraat.

✚ 7F ✉ Zuiderkerkhof ☎ 552 7977 🕓 Mon–Fri 9–4, Sat 12–4. Church
tower guided tour: Jun–Sep Wed–Sat 2, 3 and 4pm ✋ Free (church tower
inexpensive) 🚇 Nieuwmarkt, Waterlooplein 🚌 9, 14 🚢 Museum Boat
stop 3

HOTELS

De Admiraal (€)
A 17th-century spice warehouse with a nautical style makes a romantic setting for a canalside hotel. The rooms don't quite match the magical location.

✉ Herengracht 563 ☎ 626 2150 🚌 4, 9, 14

Amstel Botel (€)
Floating hotel that fits right in with Amsterdam's watery origins. Outboard rooms afford a view of the old harbour area. Facilities are modern and comfortable.

✉ Oosterdokskade 2–4 ☎ 626 4247; www.amstelbotel.com 🚇 Centraal Station 🚌 1, 2, 4, 5, 6, 9, 13, 16, 17, 24, 25

Die Port van Cleve (€€)
One-time Heineken brewery turned hotel, restored and renovated, with modern yet comfortable rooms.

✉ Nieuwezijds Voorburgwal 176–180 ☎ 718 9013; www.dieportvancleve.com 🚌 1, 2, 5, 13, 17

Estheréa (€€€)
See page 79.

De l'Europe (€€€)
Prestigious hotel combining *belle époque* architecture with opulent furnishings and the most modern amenities, in a superb riverside setting.

✉ Nieuwe Doelenstraat 2–8 ☎ 531 1777; www.leurope.nl 🚌 4, 6, 9, 14, 16, 24, 25

NH Barbizon Palace (€€€)
Luxury and a full range of modern amenities are concealed well behind the façades of a row of 17th-century houses facing Centraal Station.

✉ Prins Hendrikkade 59–72 ☎ 556 4564; www.nh-hotels.com 🚇 Centraal Station 🚌 1, 2, 4, 5, 6, 9, 13, 16, 17, 24, 25

NH Grand Hotel Krasnapolsky (€€€)

Built in the 1860s, the 'Kras' has spread through adjacent buildings, and added up-to-the-minute amenities. A highlight is the *belle époque* Wintertuin (Winter Garden) restaurant.

✉ Dam 9 ☎ 554 9111; www.nh-hotels.com 🚊 4, 9, 14, 16, 24, 25

Park Plaza Victoria Amsterdam (€€€)

The beautiful carved stone façade illustrates the class of this high-end hotel directly opposite the train station. Perfect for business travellers.

✉ Damrak 1–5 ☎ 623 4255; www.parkplaza.com 🚊 4, 9, 14, 16, 24, 25

Sint-Nicolaas (€)

If a former factory doesn't sound appealing, rest assured that this rambling place near Centraal Station has a touch of class and comfortable facilities.

✉ Spuistraat 1a ☎ 626 1384; www.hotelnicolaas.nl 🚇 Centraal Station
🚊 1, 2, 5, 6, 13, 17

Sofitel The Grand Amsterdam (€€€)

See page 79.

RESTAURANTS

Al's Plaice (€)

Never mind the painful pun, Al's traditional British fish 'n' chips are prepared by loving hands, for take-away or sit-down dining.

✉ Nieuwendijk 10 ☎ 427 4192 🕐 Mon 5–10pm, Wed–Sun noon–10pm
🚊 1, 2, 5, 6, 13, 17

De Brakke Grond (€–€€)

Flemish Cultural Centre's darkly atmospheric restaurant, serving bountiful portions of Belgian food, including *waterzooï* (chicken or fish stew) and *paling* (eel), along with the traditional steak-frites and mussels.

✉ Nes 43 ☎ 626 0044 🕐 Mon–Thu 11am–1am, Fri–Sat 11am–2am, Sun noon–1am 🚊 4, 9, 14, 16, 24, 25

Brasserie De Poort (€€)
Wooden beams and Delft blue tiles in an 1870 tavern are the backdrop for fine Dutch dining. Every thousandth steak served (they are individually numbered) comes with a free bottle of wine.

✉ Hotel Die Port van Cleve, Nieuwezijds Voorburgwal 176–180 ☎ 622 6429 🕐 Daily 7am–10:30pm 🚊 1, 2, 5, 13, 17

Brasserie Schiller (€€)
Restored, century-old *jugendstil* monument, rich in wood-panelling and etched and stained glass. Classic Dutch and international food.

✉ Hotel Schiller, Rembrandtplein 26–36 ☎ 554 0723 🕐 Daily 11–10:30 🚊 4, 9, 14, 20, 24

Breitner (€€)
Carefully prepared French dishes in a light and airy setting with a fine view over the Amstel.

✉ Amstel 212 ☎ 627 7879; www.restaurant-breitner.nl 🕐 Mon–Sat 6pm–11pm 🚊 4, 9, 14

Café Pacifico (€)
The first Mexican restaurant in the Netherlands, with a lively Latin-American atmosphere, especially on Tuesday's margarita night.

✉ Warmoesstraat 31 ☎ 624 2911; www.cafepacifico.nl 🕐 Sun–Thu 5–10:30pm, Fri–Sat 5–11pm 🚊 Centraal Station

Café Roux (€€)
See page 60.

Espresso Corner Baton (€)
Good for a quick, light lunch, this bustling place serves salads, sandwiches, quiches and more. In summer a large pavement terrace allows you to enjoy the canalside ambience.

✉ Herengracht 82 ☎ 624 8195 🕐 Mon–Fri 8–6, Sat–Sun 9–6 🚊 1, 2, 5, 6, 13, 17

Excelsior (€€€)
See page 60.

Greenwood's (€)

Cosy English tea room, serving home-made scones, with jam and clotted cream, chocolate cake and lemon meringue pie.

✉ Singel 103 ☎ 623 7071 ⏲ Daily 9:30–7 🚊 1, 2, 5, 6, 13, 17

Haesje Claes (€€)

Eight wood-beamed dining-rooms in a house from 1520, serving traditional Dutch cuisine with a 'from canapés to caviar' ethos.

✉ Spuistraat 273–275 ☎ 624 9998 ⏲ Daily noon–10 🚊 1, 2, 5

Hemelse Modder (€€)

Chocoholics will appreciate the chocolate mousse that gives 'Heavenly Mud' its name. First sample a vegetarian main course.

✉ Oude Waal 9–11 ☎ 624 3203 ⏲ Tue–Sun 6–10pm 🚇 Nieuwmarkt

De Jaren (€–€€)

See page 60.

Kantjil en de Tijger (€–€€)

'Antelope and the Tiger' spurns the colonial look and serves spicy Javanese food in a cool, modern setting.

✉ Spuistraat 291–293 ☎ 620 0994 ⏲ Daily 4:30–11pm 🚊 1, 2, 5

Lovers (€€€)

A candlelit dinner cruising on the canals, while the historic gables glide past, is almost guaranteed to be a romantic experience.

✉ Prins Hendrikkade (at Centraal Station) ☎ 530 1090 ⏲ Apr–Oct daily 7:30pm; Nov–Mar Wed, Fri, Sat 7:30pm 🚊 1, 2, 4, 5, 6, 9, 13, 16, 17, 24, 25

Luxembourg (€)

See page 61.

Memories of India (€€€)

Delicately flavoured tandoori, Moghlai and vegetarian cuisine in a setting that adopts a restrained version of Indian décor.

✉ Reguliersdwarsstraat 88 ☎ 623 5710 ⏲ Daily 5–11:30pm 🚊 4, 9, 14, 16, 24, 25

Morita-Ya (€)

Traditional Japanese snack bar that eschews the hallowed atmosphere of many Japanese restaurants in favour of a convivial local style, and serves great sushi and sashimi.

✉ Zeedijk 18 ☎ 638 0756 🕓 Tue–Sun 6–10pm 🚋 1, 2, 4, 5, 9, 13, 16, 17, 24, 25

Nam Kee (€)

Don't be fooled by the very basic décor, this is the most popular Chinese eatery in Amsterdam.

✉ Zeedijk 115 ☎ 639 2848 🕓 Daily noon–11pm 🚋 1, 2, 4, 5, 9, 13, 16

Rose's Cantina (€–€€)

Noisy place whose Tex-Mex food in a vaguely Mexican setting is unexceptional, yet whose camaraderie – and great margaritas – mean it's hard to get a table.

✉ Reguliersdwarsstraat 38–40 ☎ 625 9797 🕓 Tue–Sun 5–11:30pm 🚋 1, 2, 5

Royal Café de Kroon (€€)

See page 61.

La Ruche (€)

Take the weight off shopping-weary feet over coffee and apple pie topped with fresh cream in this department store café overlooking the Dam.

✉ De Bijenkorf, Dam 1 ☎ 552 1772 🕓 Mon–Wed 11:30–6:30, Thu–Fri 11:30–8:30, Sat–Sun 11:30–5:30 🚋 4, 9, 14, 16, 24, 25

Sea Palace (€€)

It might not have the best Chinese food in town, but eating lunch or dinner aboard a pagoda-style floating restaurant, modelled on Hong Kong's famous Jumbo restaurant, adds romance to the experience.

✉ Oosterdokskade 8 ☎ 626 4777 🕓 Daily noon–11pm 🚋 1, 2, 4, 5, 6, 9, 13, 16, 17, 24, 25

Shibli (€€€)

Sit on a sofa inside a tent amid Bedouin ornaments and rugs, dining on a sophisticated Arab banquet, and finish the whole experience with a puff of apple-and-honey tobacco from a *hookah* (water-pipe).

✉ Oudezijds Voorburgwal 236 ☎ 554 6079 🕙 Daily 7pm–midnight
🚌 4, 9, 14, 16, 24, 25

De Silveren Spiegel (€€€)

The 'Silver Mirror', in twin step-gabled houses dating from 1614, reflects good taste with sophisticated traditional Dutch cuisine enhanced by a continental tang.

✉ Kattengat 4–6 ☎ 624 6589 🕙 Mon–Sat 5:30–10:30pm
🚌 1, 2, 5, 13, 17

Tuynhuys (€€€)

Superb French/Mediterranean cuisine served in the one-time coach house of a 17th-century mansion, with dishes including Zeeland mussels, venison and wild duck.

✉ Reguliersdwarsstraat 28 ☎ 627 6603; www.tuynhuys.nl 🕙 Mon–Fri noon–2:30, daily 6–10:30pm 🚌 4, 9, 14, 16, 24, 25

D'Vijff Vlieghen (€€€€)

With seven individually decorated dining-rooms, the 'Five Flies' flits through a variety of historic Old Dutch interior styles while focusing culinary attention on producing light, sophisticated New Dutch cooking.

✉ Spuistraat 294–302 ☎ 530 4060 🕙 Daily 5:30–10pm 🚌 1, 2, 5

In de Waag (€€)

The ground floor of an old city gate and weigh house has been transformed into a restaurant with an authentic medieval look – you dine at long, candlelit benches – and are treated to a totally modern taste.

✉ Nieuwmarkt 4 ☎ 422 7772; www.indewaag.nl 🕙 Daily 10am–midnight
🚇 Nieuwmarkt

SHOPPING

ANTIQUES

Premsela & Hamburger

Dutch royalty gives its seal of approval, and its custom, to this refined setting for antique and contemporary silver and jewellery. Also does repair work.

✉ Rokin 98 ☎ 627 5454; www.premsela.com 🚌 4, 9, 14, 16, 24, 25

BOOKS

American Book Center

In addition to its mainstream books, this multi-floor store has strong specialist sections, including gay, erotic, science fiction and fantasy books, as well as second-hand magazines, war-games and sword-and-sorcery games.

✉ Spui 12 ☎ 625 5537 🚌 4, 9, 14, 16, 24, 25

Athenaeum Boekhandel

An art nouveau store from 1904 divided into a warren of nooks and crannies for mainly high-brow books in different languages. The attached Athenaeum Nieuwshandel sells international newspapers.

✉ Spui 14–16 ☎ 514 1460 🚌 1, 2, 5

De Slegte

The city's largest second-hand bookshop has a vast choice of titles in multiple languages on several floors.

✉ Kalverstraat 48–52 ☎ 622 5933 🚌 4, 9, 14, 16, 24, 25

Vrolijk Gay and Lesbian Bookstore

Large range of books, primarily in English. Often cheaper than gay sections of mainstream stores.

✉ Paleisstraat 135 ☎ 623 5142; www.vrolijk.nl 🚌 1, 2, 4, 5, 6, 9, 13, 14, 16, 17, 24, 25

Waterstone's

Branch of the British chain, with a huge stock of hardbacks and paperbacks, fiction and non-fiction, for adults and children.

✉ Kalverstraat 152 ☎ 638 3821 🚌 1, 2, 4, 5, 9, 14, 16, 24, 25

GIFTS
Gastronomie Nostalgie
An outlet for antique kitchen- and tableware of the kind once found in grand European hotels like the Ritz and the Hôtel de Paris.

✉ Nieuwezijds Voorburgwal 304 ☎ 422 6226 🚊 1, 2, 5

DEPARTMENT STORES
De Bijenkorf
Flagship, up-market department store.

✉ Dam 1 ☎ 552 1700 🚊 4, 9, 14, 16, 24, 25

Hema
Cheap 'n' cheerful bargain basement chain. Good for underwear, household goods and some food items.

✉ Kalvertoren Shopping Centre, Singel 457/A1 ☎ 422 8988 🚊 4, 9, 14, 16, 24, 25

Magna Plaza
The turreted, Gothic, former post office, known as 'Perenberg' (Pear Mountain), is now a chic mall with shops and cafés.

✉ Nieuwezijds Voorburgwal 182 ☎ 626 9199 🚊 1, 2, 5, 6, 13, 14, 17

Maison de Bonneterie
Up-market store for clothing, shoes, household goods, sports equipment and more.

✉ Kalverstraat 183/Rokin 140–142 ☎ 531 3400 🚊 4, 9, 14, 16, 24, 25

Vroom & Dreesmann
Clothing, jewellery, perfumes, electronic and household goods.

✉ Kalverstraat 203 ☎ 0900/235 8363 🚊 4, 9, 14, 16, 24, 25

FOOD AND DRINK
De Bierkoning
You ought to find something to your taste among 950 different kinds of beer from all over the world, many of which come with their own accompanying glass.

✉ Paleisstraat 125 ☎ 625 2336 🚊 1, 2, 5, 6, 13, 14, 17

Geels en Co
See pages 80–81.

Jacob Hooij
A medley of fragrant scents greets you as you enter this 1743 apothecary, selling herbs, spices, health foods and a variety of natural cosmetics.

✉ Kloveniersburgwal 12 ☎ 624 3041 🚇 Nieuwmarkt

Vitals Vitamin Advice Shop
Vitamins, minerals and a range of food supplements.

✉ Nieuwe Nieuwstraat 47 ☎ 427 4747 🚊 1, 2, 5, 6, 13, 17,

H P De Vreng en Zoon
Decorated with 15,000 miniature bottles, this distillery and liquor store has been producing *jenever* and liqueurs since 1852.

✉ Nieuwendijk 75 ☎ 624 4581 🚊 1, 2, 5, 6, 13, 17

Wout Arxhoek
One of the city's best cheese shops, with more than 250 different varieties to choose from – imported from around the world as well as Dutch.

✉ Damstraat 19 ☎ 622 9118 🚊 4, 9, 14, 16, 24, 25

FASHION AND ACCESSORIES
Palette
Tiny shop with a big choice of well-made shoes in satin and silk.

✉ Nieuwezijds Voorburgwal 125 ☎ 639 3207 🚊 4, 9, 14, 16, 24, 25

Weber's Holland
Sexy, humorous and avant-garde fashion, mainly for women.

✉ Kloveniersburgwal 26 ☎ 638 1777 🚇 Nieuwmarkt 🚊 4, 9, 14, 16, 24, 25

ALTERNATIVE
Absolute Danny
Erotic clothing and accessories with a sense of style.

✉ Oudezijds Achterburgwal 78 ☎ 421 0915 🚊 4, 9, 14, 16, 24, 25

Condomerie Het Gulden Vlies

This is the world's first specialist condom shop. The 'Golden Fleece' stocks an impressive range of this singular item of apparel.

✉ Warmoesstraat 141 ☎ 627 4174 🚊 4, 9, 14, 16, 24, 25

The Headshop

Market leader since the heady summer of 1968 in drug paraphernalia and books, oriental clothing, weird and wonderful jewellery, insight into magic mushrooms and more along the same lines.

✉ Kloveniersburgwal 39 ☎ 624 9061 Ⓜ Nieuwmarkt

Hemp Works

Clothing, cosmetics and more, all made from multi-purpose hemp fibre.

✉ Nieuwendijk 13 ☎ 421 1762 🚊 1, 2, 5, 6, 13, 17

BICYCLE SHOPS AND RENTAL

Mac Bike

This essential bicycle shop, close to Centraal Station, has been in business since 1988, and has two other outlets in the city. They not only rent and sell bikes, they repair them and organize guided bike tours too, and you might be able to find that bike accessory you can't find at home, or buy a fun gift for a cyclist friend.

✉ Stationsplein 5, 12 and 33 ☎ 620 0985; www.macbike.nl
Ⓜ Centraal Station

Rent-a-Bike

A bicycle may not be the typical holiday souvenir, but if you fall in love with Dutch bicycles you can get one here and have it shipped home for you. The Amsterdam sit-up city bicycles are very reasonably priced, and it would certainly be fun to have one at home!

✉ Damstraat 20–22 ☎ 625 5029; www.bikes.nl
🚊 4, 9, 14, 16, 24, 25

ENTERTAINMENT

MUSIC AND DANCE
Beurs van Berlage
Home of the Netherlands Philharmonic Orchestra and Netherlands Chamber Orchestra, in the former stock exchange.

✉ Damrak 213 ☎ 530 4141 ⏰ Box office: Tue–Fri 12:30–6, Sat 12:30–5, and 1 hour 15 minutes before performances 🚊 4, 9, 14, 16, 24, 25

Muziekgebouw
This new concert hall houses the De IJsbreker modern music centre, the Bimhuis jazz club and other musical ventures.

✉ Piet Heinkade 1 ☎ 788 2000; www.muziekgebouw.nl ⏰ Box office: Mon–Sat 12–7 🚊 IJtram, 16

Muziektheater
Home of the Netherlands Opera and National Ballet, and Amsterdam venue for performances by The Hague's highly regarded Netherlands Dance Theatre.

✉ Waterlooplein 22 ☎ 551 8117 or 551 8006 ⏰ Box office: Mon–Sat 10–6, Sun 11:30–6 🚇 Waterlooplein 🚊 IJ tram, 16

LIVE MUSIC
Bimhuis
The place for serious lovers of improvizational jazz. Now housed in the Muziekgebouw.

✉ Piet Heinkade 3 ☎ 788 2150; www.bimhuis.nl 🚊 IJtram, 16

De Heeren van Aemstel
Upper-crust café where you occasionally catch some big names at their session on Wednesday at 9:30.

✉ Thorbeckeplein 5 ☎ 620 2173 🚊 4, 9, 14

PROEFLOKAAL (TASTING HOUSE)
De Drie Fleschjes
Rows of padlocked wooden kegs line a wall in the 'Three Little Bottles', from 1650.

✉ Gravenstraat 18 ☎ 624 8443 🚊 1, 2, 4, 5, 9, 13, 14, 16, 24, 25

Canal Ring East

The east of Amsterdam is a mix of docklands, which are undergoing restoration as homes, offices and entertainment venues, and residential areas that have attracted multi-cultural settlers.

A number of the city's attractions are in this district, including the Hortus Botanicus and Nederlands Scheepvaart-museum.

Take the time, too, just to stroll along the quiet, leafy canals here.

Natura Artis Magistra

Oosterpark

OOST

AMSTELPARK

This beautiful green area, created in 1972 for a decennial national flower show, the Floriade, lies along the River Amstel on the edge of town. It is hemmed in on the north by the busy A10 ring road and on the west by suburban Buitenveldert. You can stroll around its central pond and through a rosarium and rhododendron garden, get lost in a maze, and visit the Glazenhuis (Glass House) art gallery and a children's farm. De Rieker windmill is just outside the park to the south.

➕ 21M (off map) ✉ Between Amsteldijk and Europaboulevard
🕐 Park: dawn–dusk; Glazenhuis: Mar–Nov Mon–Fri 10–5 💰 Free
🍴 Rosarium café-restaurant (€–€€) 🚌 Bus 65, 199, 248

AMSTERDAMS VERZETSMUSEUM

The Resistance Museum tells the story of Amsterdam's five years (1940–45) under Nazi occupation during World War II.

Among the events it highlights are the 1941 February Strike against the deportation of the city's Jewish population, and the terrible 'Hunger Winter' of 1944–45, as well as the minutiae of underground activities: illegal newspapers, espionage, sabotage, assassination.

➕ 21G ✉ Plantage Kerklaan 61a
☎ 620 2535 🕐 Tue–Fri 10–5, Sat–Sun and public hols 12–5. Closed 1 Jan, 30 Apr, 25 Dec 💰 Inexpensive 🚌 6, 9, 14

ARTIS

Holland's largest zoo houses more than 6,000 animals, including lions, tigers, leopards, elephants and rhinoceroses. Its full name is Natura Artis Magistra: 'Nature, Teacher of the Arts', and among its

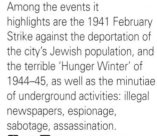

attractions are extensive gardens whose range of tree and plant varieties almost rivals that of nearby Hortus Botanicus (➤ 132). Artis does its best to replicate the animals' natural environment, using glass and perspex (plexiglass) to get you close to them. Good examples are the Reptile House, with its steamy jungle settings, and the renovated 1882 Aquarium, which has glass tanks in which seals play, as well as displays on coral reefs, the Amazon and a surprising, cut-away view of an Amsterdam canal, with fish swimming beside a sunken bicycle and other urban detritus. To get value from the steep admission price, visit, at no extra charge, the excellent Planetarium, Geological Museum and Zoological Museum. If you have young children don't let them miss the children's farm.

✚ 22H ✉ Plantage Kerklaan 38–40 ☎ 523 3400 🕓 Daily 9–5 (till 6pm Apr–Oct); Planetarium closed Mon morning ✋ Very expensive 🍴 Artis restaurant (€) 🚌 6, 9, 14 ⛴ Artis Express boat from Centraal Station

BIJLMERMEER

Until recent years, this district in the southeast of the city, and beyond the Canal Ring, was fast becoming a ghetto with crime and drug addiction rife. It reached rock bottom in 1992 when an Israeli El Al cargo aircraft crashed into a tower block, killing 43 people. Since then money has been invested to redevelop the area. This process has been aided by the opening of Ajax football club's giant Amsterdam ArenA stadium, and the Amsterdam Poort shopping, commercial and entertainment complex. The 'Bijlmer', as the district is known locally, has come up a little in the world. It's still no paradise but it adds a wider social context to a city visit.

✚ 24M (off map)

DE GOOIER (FUNENMOLEN)

Built in 1725 on a brick base with octagonal body and thatched wooden frame, one of the few surviving city windmills houses Brouwerij 't IJ, a small brewery and *proeflokaal*. It occasionally whirls into action.

✚ 24G ✉ Funenkade 7 ☎ 622 8325 🕐 Wed–Sun 3–8 🚊 7, 10 ✋ Free

HERMITAGE AMSTERDAM

Set in the rambling 17th-century Amstelhof building and annexes on the east bank of the River Amstel, this Amsterdam offshoot of St Petersburg's State Hermitage Museum won't be completed until 2009. The first phase sets the scene with a changing series of exhibitions of elements from the Russian museum's vast collection of art, fine art and crafts.

✚ 19H ✉ Neerlandia Gebouw (Building), Nieuwe Herengracht 14 ☎ 530 8755 🕐 Daily 10–5 ✋ Moderate 🚇 Waterlooplein 🚊 9, 14 🚤 Museum Boat stop 3

HOLLANDSCHE SCHOUWBURG

Only the ruined façade remains of this operetta theatre from 1892, which in 1941 became the Jewish-only Joodsche Schouwburg, an assembly point for Dutch Jews awaiting deportation to concentration camps. It is now a memorial to those 'who…did not return', with a list of deportees' family names, an eternal flame and a small museum showing items belonging to some of the 60,000 people the Nazis herded here on their way to death.

www.hollandscheschouwburg.nl

✠ 21H ✉ Plantage Middenlaan 24 ☎ 626 9945 ⏱ Daily 10–4 🖐 Free
🚌 6, 9, 14

HORTUS BOTANICUS

With 250,000 flowers and 115,000 plants and trees from more than 8,000 varieties, including rare and endangered species, the city's botanical garden has one of the world's largest collections. Founded in 1638 as the Hortus Medicus, for growing medicinal plants and herbs from the Dutch East and West Indies, Australia, South Africa and Japan, Holland's second oldest such garden, after Leiden's (1587), moved here in 1682. At the turn of the 20th century it expanded as a botanical research centre attached to Amsterdam University, and in 1987, when this role ended, went independent and has flourished ever since. This colourful, scented oasis is a great place to escape the

crowds. Highlights include the Semicircle, a replica of part of its 1682 layout; the Tri-Climate House, opened in 1993, which brings together African, South American and Mediterranean plants; the Palm House, with 300-year-old palm trees that are among the world's oldest; and the Mexico/California Desert House.

The entrance to the garden is not obvious; it is hidden behind a gatehouse opposite the Herengracht. Before starting your tour of the garden, pick up a map in English – most of the labels are in Dutch. As you would expect, the garden is busy in summer, especially at the weekend but on Sundays there is a guided tour at 3pm (small extra fee).

✚ 20G ✉ Plantage Middenlaan 2a ☎ 625 9021 ✪ Feb–Nov Mon–Fri 9–5, Sat–Sun 10–5 (till 9pm Jul–Aug); Dec–Jan Mon–Fri 9–4, Sat–Sun 10–4. Closed 1 Jan, 25 Dec ✋ Moderate 🍴 De Oranjerie (€) 🚌 9, 14

MAGERE BRUG

The famous 'Skinny Bridge', a white-painted double-drawbridge, has spanned the River Amstel since 1672. The current bridge is a 1969 replacement of an 18th-century enlargement of the original, which is said to have taken its name from two wealthy sisters, called Mager, who lived on opposite banks of the Amstel and who had the bridge built to make it easier for them to visit each other. Its name more likely comes from the original bridge being so narrow that two people could barely cross at the same time. The not-so-skinny footbridge, made of African azobe wood, is the finest of the city's 60 traditional Dutch drawbridges and a big tourist draw at night, when it is lit by hundreds of lights. You might see the bicycle-borne bridge master raising it to let boats through.

✚ 19H ✉ Between Kerkstraat and Nieuwe Kerkstraat 🚌 4

NEDERLANDS SCHEEPVAARTMUSEUM

The star turn at the Netherlands Maritime Museum is the *Amsterdam*, a full-size replica of a United East India Company sailing ship that ran aground and was lost off Hastings in 1749, which is usually tied up at the museum's wharf. However, the museum is closed until early 2009 for renovation. During this time the *Amsterdam* has been moved to a new mooring near the NEMO centre (➤ 100).

The Nederlands Scheepvaartmuseum, in a 1656 Amsterdam Admiralty arsenal, is a treasure trove of this seafaring nation's long and distinguished maritime history. In addition to replica vessels you can see an ice-breaker, a lifeboat, a herring lugger, canal barges, Holland's royal barge, last used in 1962 for Queen Juliana's silver wedding anniversary, and Greenpeace's *Rainbow Warrior*, as well as models of sailing ships, liners, warships and modern cargo vessels.

Among historical maps and charts is a bound edition of cartographer Jan Blaeu's 17th-century *World Atlas*, accompanied by marine paintings, navigational instruments, photographs, ships' equipment and other nautical bits and pieces. A particular focus is the history of the Amsterdam-based Vereenigde Oostindische Compagnie (United East India Company), founded in 1602.

✚ 9E ✉ Kattenburgerplein 1 ☎ 523 2222
🕐 Currently closed for renovation until 2010; call for latest information 👲 Expensive 🍴 Café (€)
🚌 Bus 22, 32 ⛴ Museum Boat stop 2

TROPENMUSEUM

You might not be surprised to hear an Indonesian gamelan orchestra in Amsterdam – Indonesia was a Dutch colony, after all – but how about visiting an Arab bazaar, a Bombay slum or a Bangladeshi village? You will find them all, and more, at the outstanding Tropical Museum. Though built between 1916 and 1926 as a paean of praise to Holland's empire in the East and West Indies, in the 1970s it refocused on culture, crafts and environment in the developing world. A hands-on, walk-through, realistic style makes for a fun-filled and educational visit. Imaginative temporary exhibitions and performances of non-Western music are held in the lofty, galleried main hall. Visiting the Kindermuseum TM Junior gives 6- to 12-year-olds an insight into how people from other cultures live.

✚ 23J ✉ Linnaeusstraat 2 ☎ 568 8200; Kindermuseum (reservations recommended) 568 8233 ⏱ Daily 10–5 (until 3pm 5, 24, 31 Dec). Closed 1 Jan, 30 Apr, 5 May, 25 Dec ✋ Expensive 🍴 Café-restaurant Ekeko (€–€€) 🚊 7, 9, 10, 14, 20

WERF 'T KROMHOUT

The 18th-century Kromhout Wharf, one of the city's oldest dockyards, and among few still in business, runs a museum alongside its day-to-day operations. The shipyard was founded in the 18th century by Diede Jansen Kromhout. You can watch old canal boats being repaired and see a collection of ship's engines.

✚ 22G ✉ Hoogte Kadijk 147 ☎ 627 6777 ⏱ Tue 10–3 ✋ Inexpensive 🚌 Bus 22, 43

HOTELS

Amstel InterContinental (€€€€)

On the banks of the Amstel River, this is Amsterdam's top hotel. Its 24 suites and 55 rooms are equipped with all the best facilities. The four restaurants include the Michelin-starred La Rive. The health suite includes a pool, Jacuzzi, Turkish baths and saunas.

✉ Prof Tulpplein 1 ☎ 622 6060; www.amsterdam.intercontinental.com 🚊 6, 7, 10

Club Arena (€€)

This converted 19th-century orphanage is popular with young people, with its stylish modern rooms and one of the city's hottest dance clubs, and a café-restaurant with a garden terrace.

✉ 's Gravesandestraat 51 ☎ 694 7444; www.hotelarena.nl 🚊 3, 7, 10

Prinsenhof (€)

Only a few minutes walk from Rembrandtplein, this is a good budget option – an old canal house overlooking Prinsengracht. Just 11 rooms (2 with bathrooms) with very steep stairways.

✉ Prinsengracht 810 ☎ 623 1772; www.hotelprinsenhof.com 🚊 4

Seven Bridges (€€)

In a 300-year-old house on Reguliersgracht, this is near a succession of bridges that are delightful when lit up at night. The 11 bedrooms are funished with a mix of antique and art deco items; try to get one overlooking the canal. Breakfast is served in your room.

✉ Reguliersgracht 31 ☎ 623 1329; www.sevenbridgeshotel.nl 🚊 4

RESTAURANTS

Artist Libanees Restaurant (€–€€)

Authentic Lebanese cooking; groups of five or more can order *mezes* (warm and cold appetisers) for their entire meal, otherwise you order items *à la carte*. Seats outside in summer.

✉ Tweede Jan Steenstraat 1 ☎ 671 4264; www.libanees-artist.nl 🕐 Daily 11am–1am 🚊 4, 24

Cambodja City (€)

This basic *eethuis* serves some of the finest Asian food in Amsterdam.

✉ Albert Cuypstraat 58/60 ☎ 671 4930; www.cambodjacity.nl 🕐 Tue–Sun 5–10 🚌 16, 20, 24

Dauphine (€€)

Trendy French-style bar/bistro/restaurant in chrome and steel whose name comes from one make of Renault car sold here, in what used to be a car showroom, opposite Amstel railway station. The lunch menu is predominantly burgers and steaks, though you can have lobster or oysters too, while the dinner menu is more up-market.

✉ Prins Bernardplein 175 ☎ 462 1646; www.restaurantdauphine.nl 🕐 Daily 10am–midnight (Fri–Sat till 1am) 🚌 9

De Engel (€–€€)

Grand café and balcony restaurant in a former church. Live jazz is played on Sunday afternoon and Friday night.

✉ Albert Cuypstraat 182 ☎ 675 0544; www.de-engel.net 🕐 Daily 9am–midnight 🚌 16, 20, 24

Dynasty (€€–€€€)

Smart southeast Asian restaurant in an old gabled house. If the weather is good try to get a table in the garden.

✉ Reguliersdwarsstraat 30 ☎ 626 8400 🕐 Wed–Mon 5:30–10:30 🚌 16, 24, 25

Fifteen (€€€)

This is the Amsterdam outlet of British celebrity chef Jamie Oliver's expanding chain of restaurants, set up to provide catering careers for disadvantaged youngsters. If you can get a table, this establishment is worth visiting for its location out on the Amsterdam waterfront, and its interesting Italian menu that changes weekly.

✉ Pakhuis Amsterdam, Jollemanhof 9 ☎ 0900 343 8336; www.fifteen.nl 🕐 Daily noon–1am (kitchen closes 11pm) 🚌 16, 26

Girassol (€)

The oldest and best Portuguese restaurant in town.

✉ Weesperzijde 135 ☎ 692 3471; http://girassol.nl ◷ Mon–Fri 12–3, daily 6–10 🚊 6, 7, 10

Golden Temple (€–€€)

Vegetarian food finds its rightful place here in a heavenly setting. Indian, Arab and Mexican dishes.

✉ Utrechtsestraat 126 ☎ 626 8560 ◷ Daily 5–9:30 🚊 4

Okura Hotel (€€€)

The best Japanese food in Holland is served at the Okura's Yamazato and Teppanyaki restaurants. For *sushi* and *tempura*, head to Yamazato. Teppanyaki is popular with those who want to show Japanese visitors how special is the cuisine here. While you are here don't miss the view from the 23rd-floor bar.

✉ Ferdinand Bolstraat 333 ☎ 678 8351 ◷ Yamazato: daily 7:30–9:30, noon–2, 6–9:30. Teppanyaki: daily 6–11:30

Proeflokaal Janvier (€€)

In the crypt of a 17th-century wooden church, the menu mainly comprises classic French dishes.

✉ Amstelveld 12 ☎ 626 1199; www.proeflokaaljanvier.nl ◷ Daily 12–3, 6–10 🚊 4

Sal Meijer's (€)

For the finest kosher snacks and sandwiches in town, head for Amsterdam South and this focal point of the city's Jewish community. Or call and ask about a delivery to your hotel.

✉ Scheldestraat 45 ☎ 673 1313 ◷ Sun–Thu 10–8, Fri 10–2 🚊 25

Tempo Doeloe (€€)

Although served on fine china atop linen tablecloths, a few of the *rijsttafel* dishes here can be as fiery as Krakatoa erupting. Don't let that put you off trying some of the city's best Indonesian dining.

✉ Utrechtsestraat 75 ☎ 625 6718 ◷ Daily 6–11:30pm 🚊 4, 6, 7, 10

Le Zinc…et les Autres (€€)

Hearty portions of provincial French cuisine in a wood-beamed canalside warehouse converted to a fashionably comfortable restaurant.

✉ Prinsengracht 999 ☎ 622 9044; www.lezinc.nl ⏰ Mon–Sat 5:30–11 🚊 4

ENTERTAINMENT

CINEMA, THEATRE AND CHAMBER MUSIC

De Kleine Komedie

Built in 1786, the Komedie is the oldest theatre in Amsterdam and still offers a mix of mostly cabaret and comedy, for which your Dutch had better be good, though there are some music evenings too. A very authentic Amsterdam experience.

✉ Amstel 56–58 ☎ 624 0534; www.dekleinekomedie.nl ⏰ Box office: Mon–Sat noon–6, and before shows 🚊 4, 9, 14, 16, 24, 25

Koninklijk Theater Carré

Former circus building, now staging Dutch versions of big-name musicals, cabaret, pop music, opera and ballet.

✉ Amstel 115–125 ☎ 524 9414 ⏰ Box office: daily 4–8pm; phone lines 9–9 🚇 Weesperplein 🚊 4, 6, 7, 10

Tonight

Housed in a former chapel and not too far from the centre, this club plays music from different decades on different nights. It's usually only open at weekends. The complex also has a café and hotel.

✉ s'Gravesandestraat 51 ☎ 850 2400; www.hotelarena.nl 🚊 3, 7, 10

Tuschinski Theater

Superb, art deco cinema complex with six screens. In July and August there are guided tours on Sunday and Monday at 10:30am.

✉ Reguliersbreestraat 26–34 ☎ 0900 1458 (premium rate) 🚊 4, 9, 14, 20

Canal Ring West

The Jordaan is the heart of this part of Amsterdam, and this former working-class area has become one of the city's most desirable addresses.

To orientate yourself, take a canal ride before exploring the streets where intellectual life is stimulated in the cafés and bars that are thriving here.

It is here that you can visit Anne Frank Huis, see Westerkerk and enjoy the entertainments around Leidseplein.

JORDAAN

OUD WEST

ANNE FRANK HUIS

Best places to see, ➤ 38–39.

BIJBELS MUSEUM

The Biblical Museum's twin canal houses,
with richly decorated neck-gables and a
courtyard with an ornamental garden, are
worth visiting for their intrinsic interest.
They were built in 1662 by architect Philips
Vingboons for wealthy merchant Jacob
Cromhout. In 1717, Jacob de Wit painted the
main hall's ceiling with classical scenes. The
collection focuses on life in the Holy Land
during biblical times and on Judaism and
Christianity through the centuries. Objects
on view include a model of ancient
Jerusalem, models of the temples of
Solomon and Herod, one of them dating
from 1730, a model of the Tabernacle from

1851, and archaeological finds and paintings of biblical scenes. Bibles include the first one printed in the Low Countries, in 1477, and a first edition of the authorized Dutch translation from 1637.
✚ 16G ✉ Herengracht 366–368 ☎ 624 2436 🕐 Mon–Sat 10–5, Sun and public hols 11–5. Closed 1 Jan, 30 Apr ✋ Expensive 🚊 1, 2, 5 ⛴ Museum Boat stop 4

CLAES CLAESZHOF

Wealthy cloth merchant Claes Claeszoon Anslo founded this almshouse in 1615. It is really two *hofjes*, whose tiny houses surrounding two little courtyards are now utilized as music students' homes. You can visit the courtyards when the outer door is open.

🕇 4D ✉ Egelantiersstraat 18–50/Eerste Egelantiersdwarsstraat 1–3 🖐 Free 🚃 6, 13, 14, 17

DE EILANDEN (THE ISLANDS)

Along the IJ waterfront's southern shore, redevelopment is transforming artificial islands that once held harbour installations, boat repair yards and warehouses. On the Western Islands of Prinseneiland, Bickerseiland and Realeneiland, northwest of Centraal Station, old warehouses are now desirable apartments. On KNSM Eiland, east of Centraal Station, modern apartments replace cargo-handling facilities.

🕇 5A ✉ IJ waterfront 🚃 3; bus 18, 22, 32, 35, 39, 59

DE JORDAAN

The Jordaan, which lies west of the centre
between Prinsengracht, Brouwersgracht,
Singelgracht and Leidsegracht, is a town
within a town, built for Golden Age artisans
and tradesmen who provided services to their
'betters' on the adjacent *grachtengordel*. Its
houses are smaller and more crammed

together, its waterways narrower and less grand, than those of the prestigious ring canals. The name may come from the French *jardin*, after the gardens of Protestant Huguenot refugees who lived in the area. Though infiltrated by gentrifiers, the neighbourhood retains a sense of place, and its iconoclastic working-class attitudes have been complemented by an influx of artists, designers and offbeat folks in general. With few 'sights' in the accepted sense, the Jordaan is worth visiting for its character, cafés and restaurants and individualistic shops.

✚ 4D ✉ Between Prinsengracht, Brouwersgracht, Lijnbaansgracht and Leidsegracht 🚌 1, 2, 5, 6, 7, 10, 13, 14, 17 🚢 Museum Boat stop 7

KEIZERSGRACHT

The Emperor's Canal is named for Emperor Maximilian of Austria, whose crown graces the Westerkerk spire (► 55), and has a wealth of gable and façade styles. Its 2.8km (1.7-mile) course takes in several sights that merit a close-up look. In its northern reaches, at Nos 40–44, are the Groenland Pakhuizen from 1641, three surviving warehouses from the original five in which the Greenland Company stored whale oil. Number 123, the Huis met de Hoofden, has six sculpted heads on the façade, representing Greek gods. Near the canal's southern end is the Museum Van Loon (► 162–163).

✚ 4F 🍴 Bars, cafés and restaurants (€–€€€) 🚌 1, 2, 4, 5, 6, 13, 14, 16, 17, 24, 25 🚢 Museum Boat stop 4, 7

LEIDSEPLEIN

Best places to see, ➤ 44–45.

NOORDERKERK

The austere North Church, renovated in 1997 and 1998, is a rarity in this nominally Calvinist city: a Calvinist church with a substantial congregation. It was built in the shape of a Greek cross by Hendrick de Keyser, and completed in 1623 by Hendrick Staets after De Keyser's death in 1621. Staets tucked four little triangular houses into the angles of the cross. Surrounding Noordermarkt hosts a bird market and organic food market on Saturday with stalls selling fruit and vegetables, herbs and cheeses, and a flea market on Monday.

➕ 4C ✉ Noordermarkt 44–48 ☎ 626 6436 ⏱ Apr–Oct Mon and Wed 10:30–3, Thu and Sat 11–1, Sun 1:30–5:30 💵 Free 🚌 Bus 18, 22

PRINSENGRACHT

Best things to do, ➤ 71.

SINT-ANDRIESHOFJE

Bequeathed in 1615–17 by cattle farmer Ivo Gerrittszoon, this restored almshouse still forms a social housing unit. A corridor lined with Delft blue tiles leads to a courtyard garden, filled with flowers and containing a water pump and a dedication stone with the legend *Vrede Sy Met U* (Peace Be With You).

➕ 3D ✉ Egelantiersgracht 107–145 🚌 7, 10, 17

STEDELIJK MUSEUM BUREAU AMSTERDAM

The decision by the Stedelijk Museum to focus on displaying modern art up to about the 1970s has left space in its coverage – or a window of opportunity – between that decade and the present which this 'offspring' gallery is designed to fill. It does so by focusing on contemporary painting, sculpture, video works, installations and performance art, mainly by young Dutch artists.

✚ 3E ✉ Rozenstraat 59 ☎ 422 0471; www.smba.nl 🕐 Tue–Sun, public hols 11–5. Closed 1 Jan, 30 Apr, 25 Dec ✋ Free 🚋 13, 14, 17, 20; bus 21, 170, 171, 172

THEATERMUSEUM

Housed in a 1638 canalside mansion designed by Philips Vingboons, with 18th-century painted ceilings by Jacob de Wit and other artists, the museum is a storehouse of Dutch and international theatre, as well as a fine example of a patrician canal house. You can see a miniature stage, costumes, models, masks, puppets, photographs, paintings and theatrical backdrops. The Netherlands Theatre Institute occupies offices in the adjacent four canal houses, including the Bartolotti House at No 170–172, built in 1618 by Hendrick de Keyser, which also has ceilings by De Wit, and others.

✚ 4E ✉ Herengracht 168 ☎ 551 3300; www.tin.nl 🕐 Mon–Fri 11–5, Sat–Sun and public hols 1–5. Closed 1 Jan, 30 Apr, 25 Dec ✋ Inexpensive 🍴 Café (€) 🚋 13, 14, 17 🚤 Museum Boat stop 7

WESTERKERK

Best places to see, ➤ 54–55.

WESTINDISCH HUIS

Opened in 1615 as a meat market, in 1623 this became headquarters of the Dutch West India Company, which controlled Holland's trade with the Americas. In the same year the company built a settlement on Manhattan Island and in 1626 founded Nieuw Amsterdam (New York), naming nearby districts after Haarlem (Harlem), Breukelen (Brooklyn) and the Dutch republic's parliament, the Staten-Generaal (Staten Island). A statue of Peter Stuyvesant, Nieuw Amsterdam's governor from 1646 until 1664, stands in the courtyard, and the building now houses the John Adams Institute, a US-orientated literary and philosophical society.

✚ 5C ✉ Herenmarkt (entrance at Haarlemmerstraat 75) 🚋 1, 2, 5, 6, 13, 17; bus 18, 22

WOONBOOTMUSEUM (HOUSEBOAT MUSEUM)

If you've ever wondered what life is like aboard the city's 2,500 houseboats moored on the canals, the River Amstel and in the harbour, the Houseboat Museum is your chance to find out – though as houseboats are as individual as the people who live on them, it can only be an example rather than typical.

The 23m (75ft) *Hendrika Maria*, built in 1914, was a working canal barge before being converted to a houseboat. Its hold is now living space, together with the deckhouse where the skipper and his family lived. You can tour these quarters, which have models and photographs on view, although it's hard to stand up straight.

www.houseboatmuseum.nl

🕆 3F ✉ Beside Prinsengracht 296 ☎ 427 0750 🕐 Mar–Oct Tue–Sun 11–5; Nov–Feb Fri–Sun 11–5. Closed 1 Jan, 30 Apr, 25–27 Dec 👆 Inexpensive 🚌 6, 13, 14, 17 ⛴ Museum Boat stop 7

See a houseboat inside

HOTELS

Acacia (€)

Small Jordaan hotel owned by an enthusiastic couple who keep it comfortable and friendly. Also rooms on nearby houseboats.

✉ Lindengracht 251 ☎ 622 1460; www.hotelacacia.nl 🚌 3, 10

Belga (€)

Backpackers' *pied-à-terre*, with large rooms suitable for multiple occupancy and a friendly, family-owned style that complements the 17th-century building.

✉ Hartenstraat 8 ☎ 624 9080; www.hotelbelga.nl 🚌 1, 2, 5, 6, 13, 14, 17

Pulitzer (€€€)

A real prizewinner, spread through two dozen 17th- and 18th-century canal houses with gardens. Facilities among the bare brick and oak beams are generally modern and stylish.

✉ Prinsengracht 315–331 ☎ 523 5235; www.pulitzer.nl 🚌 6, 13, 14, 17

RESTAURANTS

Akbar (€€)

Akbar's consistently good curries, tandoori and other dishes don't let Indian cuisine down.

✉ Korte Leisedwarsstraat 15 ☎ 624 2211 🕐 Daily 4:30pm–12:30am
🚌 1, 2, 5, 6, 7, 10

Amsterdam (€€)

A handsomely renovated 19th-century water-pumping station is the scene for a cool restaurant. Continental dishes.

✉ Watertorenplein 6 ☎ 682 2666; www.caferestaurantamsterdam.nl
🕐 Daily 10:30am–midnight (till 1am Fri–Sat) 🚌 10

De Belhamel (€€€)

Art nouveau décor and classical music set the tone for polished continental cuisine, and game in season, in an intimate setting with a superb canal view.

✉ Brouwersgracht 60 ☎ 622 1095; www.belhamel.nl 🕐 Daily dinner
🚌 1, 2, 5, 6, 13, 17

Bolhoed (€€)

Two candlelit canalside rooms enlivened with ethnic art, and hard
to beat for the adventurous vegetarian recipes.

✉ Prinsengracht 60–62 ☎ 626 1803 🕐 Daily noon–10 (till 11pm Sat)
🚊 6, 13, 14, 17

Bordewijk (€€–€€€)

Deft Mediterranean and Asian culinary touches combine with
minimalist décor, adding a modern slant to French dining.

✉ Noordermarkt 7 ☎ 624 3899 🕐 Tue–Sun 6:30–10:30
🚊 1, 2, 5, 6, 13, 17

Café Américain (€€)

See page 60.

Christophe (€€€)

Chef Jean Christophe combines French sensibility with a dash of
American seasoning to good effect in his chic canalside restaurant.

✉ Leliegracht 46 ☎ 625 0807 🕐 Tue–Sat 6:30–10:30
🚊 6, 13, 14, 17, 20

Duende (€)

Dark, bustling *tapas* café, popular with Spanish expats, with a
large choice of *tapas* – hot and cold snacks.

✉ Lindengracht 62 ☎ 420 6692 🕐 Mon–Fri 5–11, Sat–Sun 4–11
🚊 1, 2, 5, 6, 13, 17

Het Land van Walem (€€)

Set aside the latest interior design and an urbane menu, and you
may find the two terraces to be its chief selling point.

✉ Keizersgracht 449 ☎ 625 3544 🕐 Daily 10am–1am (till 2am Fri–Sat)
🚊 1, 2, 5

Metz (€)

Department store English style café with a view.

✉ Metz & Co, Keizersgracht 455/Leidsestraat 34–36 ☎ 520 7020
🕐 Daily 10–5 🚊 1, 2, 5

Pasta e Basta (€€)

Very popular partly because of its chi-chi Italian food and partly because the members of staff are liable to burst into live opera.

✉ Nieuwe Spiegelstraat 8 ☎ 422 2222 🕐 Daily 6–11pm
🚍 16, 24, 25

De Prins (€)

Bustling brown café with an above-average, small busy restaurant, and with a daily changing menu of Dutch and French dishes.

✉ Prinsengracht 124 ☎ 624 9382 🕐 Daily 10–10 🚍 6, 13, 14, 17

De 2 Grieken (€€)

This family-run Greek bistro is famous for its mountain goat stew and mixed grills.

✉ Prinsenstraat 20 ☎ 625 5317 🕐 Daily 5–11pm 🚍 6, 13

SHOPPING

ANTIQUES
Kunst–Antiekcentrum De Looier

Rambling art and antiques market in a collection of warehouses, with 160-plus dealers selling anything from heirlooms to collectable gewgaws.

✉ Elandsgracht 109 ☎ 624 9038; www.looier.nl 🚍 7, 10, 17

ART
Amsterdam Smallest Gallery

Near the Anne Frank House you can visit this tiny gallery, which specializes in beautiful and striking city and Dutch scenes by artist/owner Sonja.

✉ Westermarkt 60 ☎ 622 3756; www.smallestgallery.com 🚍 13, 14, 17

GIFTS
BLGK

Showcase for a group of local jewellery designers, each one with a different contemporary approach, but all making a variety of notable pieces at reasonable prices.

✉ Hartenstraat 28 ☎ 624 8154 🚍 6, 13, 14, 17

Blue Gold Fish
Fantastical gifts of all sorts, including jewellery, ornaments, fabrics and other items that don't fall into any easily defined category.
✉ Rozengracht 17 ☎ 623 3134 🚊 6, 13, 14, 17

Galleria d'Arte Rinascimento
This slightly eccentric shop sells both the finest De Porcelyne Fles Delftware, and cheap imitations.
✉ Prinsengracht 170 ☎ 622 7509 🚊 6, 13, 14, 17

Heinen
Hand-painted De Koninklijke Fles Delft Blue and Tichelaars Makkumware, made by a father-and-son team of craftsmen.
✉ Prinsengracht 440 ☎ 627 8299 🚊 1, 2, 5, 13, 17

CHILDREN'S CLOTHES AND TOYS
Mechanisch Speelgoed
Batteries definitely not included in these modern versions of toys from a kinder, gentler era of youthful playthings.
✉ Westerstraat 67 ☎ 638 1680 🚊 3, 10

Pas-Destoel
Brings interior design skills and a sense of fun to bear on children's furniture, room fittings and accessories.
✉ Westerstraat 260 ☎ 420 7542 🚊 3, 10

DEPARTMENT STORE
Metz & Co
This *belle époque* building hosts a quality store with an avant-garde past, though its Rietveld furniture is now reproduction.
✉ Keizersgracht 455/Leidsestraat 34–36 ☎ 520 7020 🚊 1, 2, 5

FOOD AND DRINK
J G Beune
Sells chocolate versions of *Amsterdammertjes* (the posts that stop cars from parking on the pavement) and a colourful array of cakes.
✉ Haarlemmerdijk 156–158 ☎ 624 8356 🚊 1, 2, 5, 6, 13, 17

Eichholtz
Highly regarded delicatessen with Dutch, American and other international specialities.

✉ Leidsestraat 48 ☎ 622 0305 🚊 1, 2, 5

Patisserie Pompadour
A vast selection of delectable cakes and pastries, and an elegant tea room in which to consume those that you don't take away.

✉ Huidenstraat 12 ☎ 623 9554 🚊 1, 2, 5

FASHION AND ACCESSORIES
Cora Kemperman
Elegant and imaginative, individually designed women's fashion.

✉ Leidsestraat 72 ☎ 625 1284 🚊 1, 2, 5

Hester van Eeghen
Imaginatively designed leather accessories.

✉ Hartenstraat 37 ☎ 626 9212 🚊 6, 13, 14, 17

Sissy-Boy
A Sissy-Boy label would be quite a gift for the right friend, and this stylish but inexpensive clothing chain can be found throughout the Netherlands, with casual clothes for both men and women.

✉ Leidsestraat 15 ☎ 623 8949; www.sissy-boy.nl 🚊 1, 3, 5

HOUSEHOLD
Wonen 2000
You likely won't be able to carry away many of the larger items from this vast depository of designer furniture, but the range of portable accessories is extensive too.

✉ Rozengracht 219–223 ☎ 521 8712 🚊 6, 13, 14, 17

SPECIALITY
Cortina Paper
The paper chase ends here, in a stockpile of fine paper, including handmade, as well as writing and sketching materials.

✉ Reestraat 22 ☎ 623 6676 🚊 6, 13, 14, 17

Ivy

For a special and elegant bouquet of flowers that's more (much more) than the traditional bunch of 10 tulips.

✉ Leidseplein 35 ☎ 623 6561 🚊 1, 2, 5, 6, 7, 10

De Witte Tandenwinkel

Typical of the quirky Amsterdam shops that specialize in one thing only, this is devoted to teeth – buy fun brushes for the kids, and the latest toothbrush technology for yourself.

✉ Runstraat 5 ☎ 623 3443; www.dewittetandenwinkel.nl 🚊 1, 2, 5, 13, 14, 16, 17, 24

ENTERTAINMENT

CINEMA
City

Seven screens just off Leidseplein.

✉ Kleine Gartmanplantsoen 13–25 ☎ 0900 9363 (premium rate) 🚊 1, 2, 5, 6, 7, 10

THEATRE AND DANCE
Boom Chicago

Comedy and improv venue (all in English). Bar and restaurant.

✉ Leideseplein 12 ☎ 423 0101 🚊 1, 2, 5, 6, 7, 10

LIVE MUSIC
Melkweg

Apart from live bands most nights in this former dairy building, there are theatre performances and film shows as well as dance.

✉ Lijnbaansgracht 234a ☎ 531 8181 🚊 1, 2, 5, 6, 7, 10

Paradiso

See page 77.

COFFEE SHOP
Bulldog

Main outlet of a chain of bars and smoking coffee shops.

✉ Leideseplein 13–17 ☎ 627 1908 🚊 1, 2, 5, 6, 7, 10

Museum Quarter

Amsterdam's artistic centre is here, south of its medieval core, and largely grouped in Museumplein bordering Vondelpark. Here are the Rijksmuseum and Van Gogh Museum – repositories of treasures that will draw you here again and again.

Vondelpark is the city's largest park, and invites gentle strolling, but you can enjoy live entertainment, or refreshments. Alternatively, buy picnic ingredients, spread a rug and soak up the sun.

Vondelpark

OUD-ZUID   DE PIJP

AMSTERDAMSE BOS

It looks natural, but Amsterdam Wood is man-made.
Amsterdammers come to this 900ha (2,200-acre) forested park
on the city's southern edge for fresh air and to escape from the
city. Many bring a picnic when the weather is fine. With its trees
and plants firmly established in what was once open *polder*
(low-lying reclaimed land), the park is home to birds, insects and
small animals, and its lakes and wetland zones attract water
birds. Trace its history and learn about the plants and wildlife at
the Bezoekerscentrum (Visitor Centre).

The list of open-air activities is lengthy. In addition to a bicycle-
rental kiosk beside the main entrance, there are stables where
you can rent horses and tour the park on bridle-paths, sports
facilities, children's play areas, picnic tables, an open-air theatre,
a goat farm, boating, rowing competitions on the 2km (1.2-mile)
Roeibaan lake, and more.

In summer, take a tram ride on an antique car from the
Electrische Museumtramlijn at Haarlemmermeerstation
(➤ 162), and on Sundays and holidays, in good weather, a little
ferryboat makes trips across the Nieuwe Meer (New Lake).

✠ 13M (off map) ✉ Main entrance: Amstelveenseweg. Visitor Centre:
Bosbaanweg 5 ☎ Visitor Centre: 545 6100 🕐 Park: always open;
Visitor Centre: daily 12–5 ✋ Free 🍴 De Bosbaan café, De Manegerie
café (€–€€) 🚌 Bus 170, 171, 172

COBRA MUSEUM

Begun in 1948, the CoBrA group took its name from the founding artists' home cities: Copenhagen, Brussels and Amsterdam. In creating a new, post-war art, they reached for childlike, spontaneous imagery, often executed in bold colours with crayon, that laid the foundations of abstract expressionism. Their first exhibition, at Amsterdam's Stedelijk Museum (➤ 110–111) in 1949, ignited fierce controversy. CoBrA has since become more accepted and now has this permanent home. Vividly expressionistic works by Karel Appel, Asger Jorn and Pierre Alechinsky are among those on display at the dazzlingly white museum in respectable, suburban Amstelveen.

www.cobra-museum.nl

✚ 16M (off map) ✉ Sandbergplein 1–3, Amstelveen ☎ 547 5050
🕐 Tue–Sun 11–5. Closed 1 Jan, 1 Apr, 30 Apr, 25 Dec ✋ Moderate
🍴 Café-restaurant (€) 🚃 51 Amstelveen 🚌 5

CONCERTGEBOUW

Classical musicians consider the home of the Koninklijke Concertgebouworkest (Royal Concertgebouw Orchestra), which opened in 1888, to be one of the world's most acoustically perfect concert halls. Architect Adolf van Gendt designed it in neo-Dutch renaissance style with a neoclassical colonnade. Portrait busts of Beethoven, Sweelinck and Bach greet you at the entrance, and a sculpted lyre adorns the roof. There are two performance halls, the Grote Zaal (Grand Hall) and the Kleine Zaal (Little Hall), which is used for recitals.

🚇 15K 📧 Concertgebouwplein 2–6 ☎ 671 8345 🕐 Box office daily 10–5; 8:15 for tickets same day ✋ Lunchtime concerts free; otherwise moderate to expensive 🍴 Café (€) 🚋 3, 5, 12, 16 ❓ Guided tours by prior arrangement Sun 9:30 (only for those attending the concert afterwards)

COSTER DIAMONDS

This is one of the several quality diamond workshops in the city to offer guided tours. Amsterdam got into the diamond business around 1586, when diamond-workers and traders from Bruges and Antwerp, many of whom were Jewish, fled to the city to escape the Spanish Inquisition. Such famous diamonds as the Cullinan and Koh-I-Noor were cut in Amsterdam. Coster's 30-minute tour includes a brief history of diamonds, and it is fascinating to watch the company's craftspeople at work, cutting, polishing, sorting and setting.

🚇 19J 📧 Paulus Potterstraat 2–6 ☎ 305 5555 🕐 Daily 9–5. Closed 25 Dec ✋ Free 🚋 2, 5, 20 🛥 Museum Boat stop 6

ELECTRISCHE MUSEUMTRAMLIJN AMSTERDAM

Not only has this museum, housed in the old Haarlemmermeer-station, preserved some of Amsterdam's antique trams, it has also gathered up venerable trams from other European cities. On Sundays in summer, one of these old bone-shakers sees action on the Museum Tramlijn, a 6km (4-mile) line that runs from the station southwards through the Amsterdamse Bos (➤ 158) to Bovenkerk.

www.museumtram.nl

✚ 13M (off map) ✉ Amstelveenseweg 264 ☎ 673 7538 🕔 Apr–Oct Sun and public hols 11–5; Jul–Aug also Wed (call or check website for times) 🖐 Inexpensive 🚌 16, 24

HEINEKEN EXPERIENCE AMSTERDAM

The old Heineken brewery from 1868 hung up its mash-staff in 1988 and reopened two years later as a museum. The high-tech, high-energy, multimedia, hands-on series of interactions has undergone extensive renovations.

www.heinekenexperience.com

✚ 17K ✉ Stadhouderskade 78 ☎ 523 9666 🕔 Call or check website for latest information 🚌 16, 24, 25 ❓ Over 18s only

MUSEUM VAN LOON

Along with its neighbouring twin at No 674, this classical mansion of the fading Golden Age by architect Adriaan Dortsman was built between 1671 and 1672 for two wealthy merchant brothers. Rembrandt's student, the artist Ferdinand Bol (1616–80), lived here. The Van Loon family, whose ancestors had played a distinguished role in Holland's history, bought the house in 1884, and it was transformed into a museum in the 1960s. You can visit its magnificently furnished rooms, see the many family portraits, climb the marble staircase, stroll in the garden – an oasis of peace and quiet – and admire a coach house in the shape of a Greek temple.

➕ 18H ✉ Keizersgracht 672 ☎ 624 5255 🕐 Wed–Mon 11–5. Closed 1 Jan, 30 Apr, 25 Dec 👋 Moderate 🚌 16, 24, 25

RIJKSMUSEUM
Best places to see, ➤ 48–49.

VAN GOGH MUSEUM
Best places to see, ➤ 50–51.

VONDELPARK
Best places to see, ➤ 52–53.

HOTELS

American (€€€)
Fanciful mix of Venetian Gothic and art nouveau distinguishes this hotel. The art deco Café Américain is a city landmark (➤ 60).
✉ Leidsekade 97 ☎ 556 3000; www.amsterdamamerican.com
🚊 1, 2, 5, 6, 7, 10

Bilderberg Hotel Jan Luyken (€€)
Flawless and personable service in a graceful 19th-century town house with 65 rooms on a quiet street near Vondelpark.
✉ Jan Luijkenstraat 54–58 ☎ 573 0730; www.bilderberghoteljanluyken.com
🚊 2, 5

Hilton (€€€)
Room 1902 was the scene of John Lennon and Yoko Ono's love-in. Lunches and breakfasts, together with Roberto's restaurant.
✉ Appollolaan 138 ☎ 710 6000; www.amsterdam.hilton.com 🚊 16

Stayokay Amsterdam Vondelpark (€)
A big hostel built around an older one, adding modern options.
✉ Zandpad 5, Vondelpark ☎ 589 8996; www.stayok.nl 🚊 1, 2, 5, 6, 10

Van Ostade Bicycle Hotel (€)
Small, well-kept place that also rents bicycles and dispenses maps.
✉ Van Ostadestraat 123 ☎ 679 3452; www.bicyclehotel.com
🚊 3, 12, 24, 25

RESTAURANTS

An (€)
Basic, inexpensive Japanese eatery. Choose from sushi to teriyaki.
✉ Weteringschans 76 ☎ 624 4672; www.japansrestaurantan.nl 🕐 Tue–Sat 6–10pm 🚊 6, 7, 10

De Knijp (€€)
Near the Concertgebouw; dine here on French and Dutch dishes.
✉ Van Baerlestraat 134 ☎ 671 4248; www.deknijp.nl 🕐 Mon–Fri noon–3; daily 5:30pm–12:30am 🚊 3, 5, 12, 16, 24

Mangerie de Kersentuin (€€–€€€)

Dishes from around the world adapted to Dutch ingredients.

✉ Bilderberg Garden Hotel, Dijsselhofplantsoen 7 ☎ 570 5600 🕙 Mon–Fri 12–2, Mon–Sat 6–10 🚊 5, 16, 24

Wildschut (€–€€)

A chic, art deco bistro that attracts an arts and media crowd and serves up international dishes from BLTs through pasta to 'surf and turf'.

✉ Roelof Hartplein 1–3 ☎ 676 8220 🕙 Mon–Thu 9am–1am, Fri 9am–3am, Sat 10:30am–1am, Sun 9:30am–midnight 🚊 3, 5, 12, 24

ENTERTAINMENT

MUSIC

Concertgebouw

Home of the famed Royal Concertgebouw Orchestra (➤ 160–161). Its Grote Zaal is considered one of the world's most acoustically perfect concert halls. Free concerts Wednesdays at 12:30.

✉ Concertgebouwplein 2–6 ☎ 671 8345; www.concertgebouw.nl 🕙 Box office: daily 10–5 for advance purchase 🚊 3, 5, 12, 16

THEATRE AND DANCE

Stadsschouwburg

Mainstream Dutch theatre, and an occasional touring performance in English. Also hosts opera and dance.

✉ Leidseplein 26 ☎ 624 2311; www.ssba.nl 🕙 Mon–Sat 12–6, Sun and public hols from 90 mins before performance 🚊 1, 2, 5, 6, 7, 10

CINEMA

Nederlands Filmmuseum

The interior of this parkland pavilion includes the Cinema Parisien. This venerable cinema was facing demolition so it was removed to this location inside the film museum. The daily screenings range from silents from cinema's early days, to contemporary movies. On July and August evenings, outdoor screenings are free.

✉ Vondelpark 3 ☎ 589 1400 🚊 1, 3, 12

Excursions

The Netherlands is a small country. From Amsterdam you can reach its farthest mainland extremities in about three hours by way of vigorous driving or an intercity train. Within easy reach of the capital, a variety of excellent excursion options awaits you. A mere 15 minutes by train from Centraal Station is Haarlem, a memorable city in its own right, and it would be hard to imagine urban experiences more varied than those offered by The Hague, Rotterdam and Utrecht. If you need to be beside water you can choose from a string of North Sea beach resorts, such as nearby Zandvoort, or the constellation of historic towns and villages encircling the IJsselmeer lake, the former Zuiderzee. You can tour around by bicycle within a fair radius of the city, or cycle to your chosen place of escape and return by train.

ALKMAAR KAASMARKT

The Cheese Market at Alkmaar, 37km (23 miles) northwest of Amsterdam, is a slice of Dutch kitsch, but no less endearing for that. Cobblestoned Waagplein is littered with heaps of round Edam and cylindrical Gouda cheeses ready for auction. You can visit the **Hollands Kaasmuseum** (Dutch Cheese Museum) in the Waag.

✉ Waagplein ⏰ Mid-Apr to mid-Sep Fri 10–12

Hollands Kaasmuseum

✉ De Waag, Waagplein 2 ☎ 072/511 4284 ⏰ Apr–Oct Mon–Thu and Sat 10–4, Fri 9–4 🖐 Inexpensive

DELFT

Home of the painter Jan Vermeer (1632–75) and burial place of Dutch royalty, Delft, 56km (35 miles) southwest of Amsterdam, is a handsome, canal-lined town. Few of its medieval buildings survived a fire in 1536 and a massive explosion at a powder magazine in 1654. Prince William the Silent, who led Holland's revolt against Spain and was assassinated in 1584 at the **Prinsenhof** is among members of the House of Oranje-Nassau buried in the 14th-century Nieuwe Kerk. Vermeer is buried in the 13th-century Oude Kerk. You can visit **De Koninklijke Porcelyne Fles,** renowned makers of hand-painted Delft blue porcelain.

🛈 Hippolytusbuurt 4 ☎ 015/215 4051; www.delft.nl ⏰ Apr–Sep Tue–Fri 9–6, Sat 10–5, Sun–Mon 10–4; Oct–Mar Tue–Sat 10–4, Sun 10–3, Mon 11–4

Prinsenhof Museum

✉ Sint-Agathaplein 1 ☎ 015/260 2358; www.prinsenhof-delft.nl ⏰ Tue–Sat 10–5, Sun and public hols 1–5. Closed 1 Jan, 25 Dec 🖐 Moderate

De Koninklijke Porcelyne Fles

✉ Rotterdamseweg 196 ☎ 015/251 2030; www.royaldelft.com ⏰ Mid-Mar to Oct daily 9–5; Nov to mid-Mar Mon–Sat 9–5. Closed 25 Dec–2 Jan 🖐 Inexpensive

EDAM

Home of the famous round, yellow-skinned cheese, Edam, 15km (9.5 miles) north of Amsterdam, lies inland along a canal from the IJsselmeer. Visit the **Edams Museum,** in a 1530s merchant's house with a floating cellar, for a look at the town's history. A cheese-making display at the Kaaswaag (Cheese-Weighing House) and the beautifully decorated Trouwzaal (Wedding Room) in the 1737 Stadhuis (Town Hall) are worth seeing. You can tour nearby cheese-making farms; leaflets are available from the VVV office.

🛈 Stadhuis, Damplein 1 ☎ 0299/315 125; www.vvv-edam.nl 🕓 Apr–Oct Mon–Sat 10–5 (Jul–Aug also Sun 12–4:30); Nov–Mar Mon–Sat 10–3

Edams Museum

✉ Damplein 8 ☎ 0299/372 644; www.edamsmuseum.nl 🕓 Apr–Oct Tue–Sat 10–4:30, Sun 1–4:30 ✋ Inexpensive

GOUDA

Gouda, renowned for its yellow-skinned, cylindrical cheese and clay pipes, is 37km (23 miles) south of Amsterdam. Its striking 15th-century Gothic **Stadhuis** (Town Hall), has a carillon whose chimes are accompanied by figures representing Count Floris V signing the town's charter in 1272. Learn the story of Gouda and cheese at the Cheese Exhibition in the **Waag** (Weigh-House), and of Gouda and pipes at the **Adrie Moerings Pottenbakkerij & Pijpenmakerij.** Visit the 16th-century Sint-Janskerk to see its superb stained-glass windows, some dating from the 1550s.

🛈 Markt 27 ☎ 0182/511 300; www.vvvgouda.nl 🕓 Mon 1–5:30, Tue–Fri 9:30–5:30, Sat 10–4

Stadhuis

✉ Markt ☎ 0182/588 758 🕓 Mon–Fri 10–12, 2–4 ✋ Inexpensive

Waag

✉ Markt 35–36 ☎ 0182/529 996 🕓 Apr–Oct Tue, Wed, Fri–Sun 1–5, Thu 10–5 ✋ Inexpensive

Adrie Moerings Pottenbakkerij & Pijpenmakerij

✉ Peperstraat 76 ☎ 0182/512 842 🕓 Mon–Fri 9–5, Sat 11–5 ✋ Free

DEN HAAG AND SCHEVENINGEN

It makes sense to visit these places together. Den Haag makes an interesting comparison with Amsterdam, having almost no canals, and being focused on government, the royal court, diplomacy and International Court of Justice. There's plenty to see, beginning with the Dutch parliament, the Binnenhof, where both chambers of the States General meet and, in its courtyard, the 13th-century Ridderzaal (Hall of the Knights), where the monarch presides over the annual state opening of parliament. You can visit Paleis Lange Voorhout, view Huis ten Bosch (home of the queen) from its surrounding park and look at Paleis Noordeinde from the street. For art, including masterpieces by Rembrandt, Vermeer and Van Gogh, visit the Mauritshuis and Haags Gemeentemuseum (Hague Municipal Museum). And there's the Omniversum Imax projection theatre; Madurodam, a miniature village; and Panorama Mesdag, a panoramic painting of Scheveningen.

Amsterdam's seaside resort, Scheveningen, can be a little ragged around the edges but it's well worth the short tram ride from The Hague to visit its superb beach hotel, the Steigenberger Kurhaus, casino, shops, good international and seafood restaurants, splendid pier and beach.

🖪 Hofweg 1 ☎ 0900/340 3505; www.denhaag.com 🕒 Mon–Fri 10–6, Sat 10–5, Sun 12–5

HAARLEM

Just 20km (12.5 miles) west of Amsterdam, this city of 150,000 is often considered to be the capital's fair little sister, with almost as much canal-fringed, Golden Age allure and far fewer everyday vexations. Founded in the 10th century, Haarlem was the seat of the medieval Counts of Holland and is today Noord-Holland's provincial capital. Its lowest ebb was a seven-month siege (1572–73) during Holland's revolt against Spain when, despite desperate resistance, the Duke of Alva's troops captured the city and massacred half its 40,000 inhabitants.

Haarlem's Grote Markt is dominated by the 80m (263ft) tower, adorned with gilt spheres, of the late-Gothic **Sint-Bavokerk** (built 1370 to 1520), also known as the Grote Kerk (Great Church). In the bright and richly ornamented interior is a 1738 Christian Müller organ, with more than 5,000 pipes, that was once played by Mozart and Handel. You can see, still embedded in the wall, a cannonball that flew through a window during the Spanish siege. The painter Frans Hals (c1580–1666), who was born in Antwerp and lived and worked in Haarlem for most of his life, is buried in the choir. In addition to such highly individualistic works as *The Gypsy Girl* and *The Laughing Cavalier*, Hals painted group portraits of the *schutters* (musketeers), local militia companies. You can see eight such works, among others, at the **Frans Halsmuseum,** including the lively *Banquet of the Officers of the St Hadrian Militia Company* (1627). The museum is in the former Oudemannenhuis, an old men's hospice from 1608.

🛈 Stationsplein 1 ☎ 0900/616 1600; www.vvvzk.nl 🕓 Apr–Sep Mon–Fri 9–5:30, Sat 10–4; Oct–Mar Mon–Fri 9:30–5, Sat 10–2

Sint-Bavokerk

✉ Oude Groenmarkt 23 ☎ 023/532 4399 🕓 Mon–Sat 10–4 💷 Inexpensive

Frans Halsmuseum

✉ Groot Heiligland 62 ☎ 023/511 5775; www.franshalsmuseum.nl
🕓 Tue–Sat 11–5, Sun and public hols 12–5. Closed 1 Jan, 25 Dec
💷 Moderate

ROTTERDAM

Rotterdam, birthplace of the humanist Desiderius Erasmus (1466–1536), began as a harbour at the end of the 14th century. 'Rotterdammers,' say the Dutch, 'are born with their sleeves already rolled up.' That helps to explain the speed with which Rotterdammers rebuilt their city, which was almost totally destroyed during World War II, and made it into what is now the world's most important harbour. The authorities decided in 1945 not to rebuild the devastated city along the old lines, launching instead a controversial experiment to create a city of the future.

Rotterdam has had all the latest trends in architecture and town planning showered on it and shows no sign of tiring. If you like modern architecture, visit the Kijkkubussen, one of a group of upended cube-shaped houses on concrete stalks; an apartment tower-block in the shape of a pencil; and an apartment building whose shape has earned it the nickname 'Paper-Clip'.

Grouped conveniently in the Museumpark are the Kunsthal (Art Hall), which mounts art and design exhibitions; Museum Boijmans Van Beuningen, whose works range from Old Masters to the day before yesterday; and the Netherlands Architecture Institute. If you want a break from touring museums, visit Blijdorp Zoo, soar above the harbour at the Euromast tower, and explore it on a Spido harbour tour boat.

🛈 Coolsingel 67 ☎ 010/271 0120; www.rotterdam.info 🕒 Mon–Thu 9–5:30, Fri 9–9, Sat 9–5:30, Sun 10–5

UTRECHT

Utrecht traces its history back to Roman times and has many memorials of its medieval role as an ecclesiastical centre. About 34km (21 miles) southeast of Amsterdam, the city has a split personality, divided between its old centre along tree-lined Oudegracht and Nieuwegracht – canals whose former warehouses have been turned into cafés and restaurants – and a modern face focused on the vast Hoog Catherijne shopping mall and Vredenburg entertainment complex.

Utrecht is dominated by the 14th-century Gothic Domtoren, 112m (367ft) high, and adjacent Domkerk (1254–1517), which stands on the site of a cathedral destroyed by a hurricane in 1647.

🛈 Domplein 9

☎ 030/236 0010; www.utrechtyourway.nl

🕓 Mon 12–6, Tue, Wed, Fri 10–6, Thu 10–8, Sat 9:30–5, Sun 12–5

VOLENDAM AND MARKEN

These two IJsselmeer resorts, 18km (11 miles) and 16km (10 miles) northeast of Amsterdam respectively, are popular with day-trippers by car, bus, bicycle and guided tour. Long-time rivals, they face each other across just 3km (2 miles) of water, presenting different faces.

Volendam, on the mainland, is Catholic, rambunctious and open; Marken, a former island connected to the mainland by a causeway in 1957, is Calvinist, tranquil and insular. In each, some local people can occasionally be seen wearing traditional costume; you're not guaranteed to see this, but you might. You can easily combine the two resorts in one trip, thereby having a chance to compare and contrast.

Volendam's focus is a long, dike-top street along the harbour, lined with souvenir shops, cafés, restaurants and fish-stalls – you might like to try the smoked IJsselmeer *paling* (eel), a speciality of the area. Marken has a harbour too, though a smaller one than at Volendam, lined with green-painted wooden houses built on stilts, some of which you can visit; others have been turned into cafés.

There are tiny hamlets scattered across the former island's *polders*, and a lighthouse stands on the shore. From mid-March to October, a tour boat connects the two resorts, sailing at half-hourly to hourly intervals on a half-hour crossing.

Between the two resorts – neutral territory, if you like – lies **Monnickendam,** which has its own busy harbour lined, also lined with cafés and restaurants, and which makes less fuss than its neighbours over its status as a tourist attraction.

🛈 Zeestraat 37, Volendam ☎ 0299/363 747; www.vvvolendam.nl

🕙 Mar–Oct Mon–Sat 10–5; Nov–Feb Mon–Sat 10–3

Monnickendam and Marken

🛈 De Zarken 2, Monnickendam ☎ 0299/651 998

🕙 Mon–Fri 9–5, Sat 9–4

along the IJsselmeer's western shore

a drive

For centuries the Zuiderzee, a stormy North Sea inlet, presented a clear and present danger to low-lying Amsterdam – so the Dutch got rid of it. In 1932, the 30km-long (18.5-mile) Afsluitdijk (Enclosing Dike) shut out the sea. In its place is the IJsselmeer, a freshwater lake and a wonderful setting for a drive through historic towns and typical Dutch scenery.

Take the A10 Amsterdam ring road east to junction 114 and follow the signs to the lake at Durgerdam. Stay on the lakeside road, heading north.

A causeway leads to Marken (➤ 175), which was once an island. Explore the pretty harbourside village on foot. You can also walk 2km (1.2 miles) to a lighthouse at the island's tip.

Re-cross the causeway and continue north on the lakeside road.

Monnickendam harbour (➤ 175) is worth visiting, though most people pass through to Volendam (➤ 175), a fishing village where you can have your picture taken wearing traditional Dutch costume. A brief detour through Edam (➤ 170) returns you to the lake.

Continue north through Warder and Scharwoude.

Take a tour around Hoorn, an historic seaport and fishing village.

Driving east and north brings you to Enkhuizen.

Visit Enkhuizen's Zuiderzeemuseum by boat. Many fields around the town are awash with tulips in spring.

Continue to Medemblik.

Visit the harbour, the steam train museum and 13th-century Kasteel Radboud (Radboud Castle).

Continue to the Afsluitdijk. Cross over to the Friesland shore or return to Amsterdam on the A7 (E22).

Distance 160km (99 miles)
Time A day
Start/end point Amsterdam
Lunch De Waag Café, Hoorn ☎ 0229/215 195

DE ZAANSE SCHANS

This living village and museum, 13km (8 miles) northwest of Amsterdam, offers a glimpse of Dutch life in times past. Set up in 1960 with relocated, green-painted Zaanstreek houses and five windmills, it's almost kitsch, but not quite, thanks to a scenic setting on the River Zaan and the interest of the trades it preserves. Shop at an 18th-century grocery store, and visit a traditional clog-maker, cheese-maker, pewter workshop, bakery museum, clock museum, working windmills and a sawmill.
www.zaanseschans.nl

✉ Zaandam ☎ 075/616 8218 🕓 Daily 9–5 💷 Site: free; museums and parking: inexpensive

ZANDVOORT

This seaside resort, 25km (15.5 miles) west of the city, is brash when it claims its place in the sun every summer, and sinks into winter melancholy by October. Whatever the weather, you can walk on the beach for an hour or so, take in the atmosphere, then retire to a café. Zandvoort's long stretch of smooth sand is lined in summer with 40 café-restaurants. There are good facilities for windsurfers, and swimming is safe, though the North Sea is generally far from warm. There is a nudist section on the beach.

Away from the beach, splurge in a different way at **Holland Casino Zandvoort,** or catch a motor or motorcycle race at Circuit Park Zandvoort. For a more leisurely experience, tour the

Kennemerduinen National Park's extensive dunes.

🛈 Schoolplein 1
☎ 023/571 7947
Holland Casino Zandvoort
✉ Badhuisplein 7 ☎ 023/574 0574 🕓 Daily 12:30pm–3am
💷 Moderate (passport and 'correct' attire needed)

HOTELS

DELFT
De Kok (€)
Stylish hotel between the railway station and the old centre.
Rooms are modern and there's a large garden with a fountain.
✉ Houttuinen 14 ☎ 015/212 2125; www.hoteldekok.nl

EDAM
De Fortuna (€–€€)
Canalside hotel in the heart of town, with a 17th-century main
building, garden and up-to-date amenities.
✉ Spuistraat 3 ☎ 0299/371 671; www.fortuna-edam.nl

DEN HAAG AND SCHEVENINGEN
Le Meridien des Indes Hotel (€€€)
Height of elegance, in an 1880s baronial mansion. Its rooms are
the last word in comfort and amenities.
✉ Lange Voorhout 54–56, The Hague ☎ 070/361 2345;
www.lemeridien.com/netherlands 🚌 1, 3, 7, 8, 9, 12

Parkhotel (€€)
Atmospheric modern hotel with modestly comfortable rooms, on
a quiet, embassy-lined street overlooking Zorgvliet Park.
✉ Molenstraat 53, The Hague ☎ 070/362 4371; www.parkhoteldenhaag.nl
🚌 7

ROTTERDAM
Bilderberg Parkhotel (€€)
Ultramodern hotel near Centraal Station, with plushly furnished
and well-equipped rooms and a garden restaurant.
✉ Westersingel 70 ☎ 010/436 3611; www.bilderberg.nl 🚌 5

New York (€€)
An 11-storey 'skyscraper' built between 1897 and 1898 as the
Holland-America Line's headquarters is now a hotel with modern
rooms and great harbour views.
✉ Koninginnenhoofd 1 ☎ 010/439 0500; www.hotelnewyork.nl 🚌 20

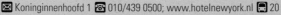

UTRECHT
Malie (€€)
Though out of the centre, this attractive small hotel in two century-old villas has room décor and furnishings that match its genteel surroundings.

✉ Maliestraat 24 ☎ 030/231 6424; www.hampshirehotels.nl 🚋 4, 11

NH Centre Utrecht (€€)
Turn-of-the-19th-century, city-centre hotel with a high standard of facilities and cosy rooms.

✉ Janskerkhof 10 ☎ 030/231 3169; www.nh-hotels.com
🚋 2, 3, 11, 12, 22

VOLENDAM
Spaander (€€)
Animated harbourside hotel that mixes old-fashioned country charm with bright, modernly furnished rooms. Pool.

✉ Haven 15–19 ☎ 0299/363 595; www.bestwestern.nl

ZANDVOORT
NH Zandvoort (€€)
Zandvoort's finest hotel offers good amenities, including a beachfront location, pool, sports facilities and modern rooms.

✉ Burgemeester van Alphenstraat 63 ☎ 023/576 0760; www.nh-hotels.com

RESTAURANTS

DELFT
Spijshuis de Dis (€€)
Steaks are the speciality and Dutch food with a touch of class is the trademark at this traditional restaurant.

✉ Beestenmarkt 36 ☎ 015/ 213 1782; www.spijshuisdedis.com
🕐 Daily 5–9:30

Stads Pannekoekhuys (€)
Traditional pancake house with 90 different kinds of pancake.

✉ Oude Delft 113–115 ☎ 015/213 0193 🕐 Apr–Sep daily 11–9; Oct–Mar Tue–Sun 11–9

EDAM
De Fortuna (€€)
The flower-bedecked canalside terrace and wood-beamed interior
are the setting for a typically Dutch menu with a dash of French.
✉ Spuistraat 3 ☎ 0299/371 671; www.fortuna-edam.nl 🕐 Mon–Sat 6–10,
Sun 5:30–10

GOUDA
Mallemolen (€€)
Canalside restaurant with Old Dutch looks and French cuisine.
✉ Oosthaven 72 ☎ 0182/515 430; www.mallemolen.com 🕐 Tue–Fri
noon–2, 5pm–midnight, Sat–Sun 5pm–midnight

DEN HAAG AND SCHEVENINGEN
't Goude Hooft (€€)
Quaint 17th-century looks disguise the effects of a 20th-century
fire. Rebuilt in the old style, with wooden beams and brass
chandeliers; great location for everything from a beer to a full
Dutch meal.
✉ Groenmarkt 13, The Hague ☎ 070/346 9713 🕐 Mon–Sat 8am–midnight,
Sun 11am–midnight

Kandinsky (€€€)
A fine restaurant with a great beachside location and sea view.
Serves superior French and Mediterranean cuisine.
✉ Steigenberger Kurhaus Hotel, Gevers Deynootplein 30, Scheveningen
☎ 070/416 2634; www.kurhaus.nl 🕐 Mon–Fri 12–3 (no lunch Jul–Aug),
6–10:30, Sat 6–10:30

HAARLEM
Jacobus Pieck (€–€€)
Stylish café-restaurant with an eclectic menu that runs from
snack-type fare at lunchtime to Dutch and international dishes
for dinner.
✉ Warmoesstraat 18 ☎ 023/532 6144; www.jacobuspieck.nl 🕐 Mon–Sat
11–4, Tue–Sat 5:30–10

De Pêcherie Haarlem aan Zee (€€)

Great seafood specialist, decked out with beach props and marine paraphernalia, and serving a menu of well-prepared fish dishes.

✉ Oude Groenmarkt 10 ☎ 023/531 4848 ◉ Mon–Sat noon–midnight, Sun 5pm–midnight

ROTTERDAM
Brasserie Henkes (€€)

A former gin distillery featuring a waterfront terrace and an old-fashioned interior. Good selection of Dutch and European dishes.

✉ Voorhaven 17 ☎ 010/425 5596 ◉ Daily 11:30am– midnight (kitchen closes at 10)

UTRECHT
Stadskasteel Oudaen (€€–€€€)

Restaurant and café set in a 14th-century canalside house. The menu leans towards Dutch and European dishes, often with a medieval slant.

✉ Oudegracht 99 ☎ 030/231 1864; www.oudaen.nl ◉ Café: daily 10am–2am; restaurant: Mon–Sat 5:30pm–9pm

VOLENDAM AND MARKEN
De Taanderij (€)

French and vegetarian dishes predominate at this refined interpretation of a traditional Dutch *eethuis*. The coffee and apple pie with cream is state of the art.

✉ Havenbuurt 1, Marken ☎ 0299/602 206 ◉ Apr–Sep daily 10–10; Oct–Mar Tue–Sun 10–10, Sun 6–10

ZAANSE SCHANS
De Hoop op d' Swarte Walvis (€€€)

Epicurean bliss on the banks of the River Zaan, with mainly French and Dutch dishes served indoors or on a riverside terrace.

✉ Kalverringdijk 15 ☎ 075/616 5629; www.dewalvis.nl ◉ Mon–Sat noon–2:30, 6–10

Sight Locator Index

This index relates to the maps on the covers. We have given map references to the main sights in the book. Some sights may not be plotted on the maps.

Index

Acknowledgements

The Automobile Association would like to thank the following photographers, companies and picture libraries for their assistance in the preparation of this book.

Abbreviations for the picture credits are as follows – (t) top; (b) bottom; (c) centre; (l) left; (r) right; (AA) AA World Travel Library

4l Canal boats, AA/A Kouprianoff; **4c** Centraal Station, AA/A Kouprianoff; **4r** Leidseplein, AA/A Kouprianoff; **5l** 't Smalle Café, AA/K Paterson; **5c** Brouwersgracht, AA/K Paterson; **5r** Delft, AA/K Paterson; **6/7** Canal boats, AA/A Kouprianoff; **8/9** Vondelpark, AA/A Kouprianoff; **10l** Prinsengracht, AA/A Kouprianoff; **10r** Van Gogh Museum, AA/ M Jourdan; **11t** Queen's Day Crowds AA/M Jourdan; **11c** Café Hoppe, AA/M Jourdan; **12** Sign, AA/K Paterson; **12/13** Street vendor, AA/A Kouprianoff; **14t** Cheese AA/M Jourdan; **14c** Beer, AA/A Kouprianoff; **14b** Waitress, AA/A Kouprianoff; **15** Herring rolls, AA/A Kouprianoff; **16/17** Barges, AA/M Jourdan; **17** Cycling AA/M Jourdan; **18** Busker, AA/M Jourdan; **19** Keukenhof, AA/M Jourdan; **20/21** Centraal Station, AA/A Kouprianoff; **25** Queen's birthday celebrations, AA/A Kouprianoff; **26/27** Centraal Station, AA/A Kouprianoff; **27** Airport. Digital Vision; **28** Canal Bus, AA/K Paterson; **34/35** Leidseplein, AA/A Kouprianoff **36t** Historical Museum, AA/K Paterson; **36b** Historical Museum, AA/K Paterson; **37** Historical Museum, AA/K Paterson; **38** Statue, AA/K Paterson; **38/39** Anne Frankhuis AA/K Paterson; **40** Beginjhof, AA/A Kouprianoff; **40/41** Beginjhof, AA/A Kouprianoff; **41** Beginjhof, AA/K Paterson; **42l** Kononklijk Paleis, AA/A Kouprianoff; **42r** Koninklijk Paleis detail, AA/K Paterson; **43** Nationaal Monument, AA/M Jourdan; **44t** Statue, van Schindel, AA/W Voysey; **44c** Giant Chess set, AA/K Paterson; **44/45** Leidseplein, AA/A Kouprianoff; **45** Leidseplein, AA/K Paterson; **46** Neon Sign, AA/M Jourdan; **47** Red Light District, AA/M Jourdan; **48t** Rijksmuseum, AA/K Paterson; **48b** Rijksmuseum, AA/K Paterson; **50** Van Gogh Painting, AA/M Jourdan; **50/51** Van Gogh Museum, AA/M Jourdan; **51** Van Gogh Museum, AA/A Kouprianoff; **52** Vondelpark, AA/A Kouprianoff; **52/53** Vondelpark, AA/A Kouprianoff; **54/55** Westekerk, AA/K Paterson; **55** Westekerk, AA/K Paterson; **56/57** 't Smalle Café, AA/K Paterson; **58** Café Hoppe, AA/M Jourdan; **61** Café, AA/A Kouprianoff; **62/63** Amsterdam view, AA/K Paterson; **64/65** Soccer, Photodisc; **66** Planetarium, AA/K Paterson; **68/69** Waterlooplein, AA/K Paterson; **70/71** Prinsengracht, AA/K Paterson; **72** Oude Kerk, AA/K Paterson; **73** Oude Kerk, AA/M Jourdan; **75** Magere Brug, AA/K Paterson; **76/77** Club, Brand X Pictures; **78** Hotel interior, AA/C Sawyer; **80/81** Shop window, AA/A Kouprianoff; **81** Carrier Bags, Stockbyte; **82/83** Brouwersgracht, AA/K Paterson; **85** Dam Square, AA/A Kouprianoff; **86** Allard Pierson Museum, AA/M Jourdan; **86/87** Beurs van Berlage, AA/A Kouprianoff; **88/89** Bloemenmarkt, AA/K Paterson; **90/91** Dam Square, AA/K Paterson; **92** Hash Museum, AA/K Paterson; **92/93** Nederlands Scheepvaartmuseum, AA/M Jourdan; **94** Jodenhoek, AA/A Kouprianoff; **95t** Joods Historisch Museum interior, JHM © Liselore Kamping; **95b** Hanukkah lamp, JHM; **96** Madame Tussaud's, AA/K Paterson; **97t** Museum Amstelkring, AA/K Paterson; **97b** Museum Amstelkring, AA/K Paterson; **98** Museum Het Rembradthuis, AA/M Jourdan; **99t** Museum Willet-Holthuysen, AA/M Jourdan; **99b** Nationaal Monument, AA/K Paterson; **100l** NEMO, AA/M Jourdan; **100r** NEMO, AA/M Jourdan; **101t** Nieuwe Kerk, AA/K Paterson; **101b** Nieuwmarkt, AA/K Paterson; **102/103** Oude Kerk, AA/K Paterson; **103t** Oude Kerk, AA/M Jourdan; **103b** Oudemanhuispoort, AA/A Kouprianoff; **104** Prinsenhof, AA/A Kouprianoff; **105** Scheepvaarthuis, AA/K Paterson; **107** Scuttersgalerij, AA/M Jourdan; **108/109** Singel, AA/K Paterson; **109** 7 Singel, AA/A Kouprianoff; **110** Sint Nicolaaskerk, AA/K Paterson; **110/111** Stedelijk Museum CS, AA/A Kouprianoff; **112/113** Waag, AA/M Jourdan; **114** Waterlooplien, AA/M Jourdan; **114** Zuiderkerk, AA/K Paterson; **127** Hortus Botanicus, AA/A Kouprianoff; **128** Verzetsmuseum interior, Verzetsmuseum; **128/129** Artis Zoo, AA/M Jourdan; **130** De Gooier, AA/M Jourdan; **131** Children, Hollandsche Schouwburg; **130/131** Hermitage Amsterdam, © Maurice Boyer; **132** Hortus Botanicus, AA/A Kouprianoff; **133** Magere Brug, AA/A Kouprianoff; **134/135** Scheepvaartmuseum, AA/K Paterson; **136** Tropenmuseum, AA/M Jourdan; **141** Jordaan, AA/A Kouprianoff; **142** Tabernakel model, Bijbels Museum; **142/143** Bijbels Museum, Bijbels Museum; **144/145** Western Isles, AA/A Kouprianoff; **146** De Jordaan, AA/A Kouprianoff; **146/147** De Jordaan, AA/K Paterson; **150** Woonbootmuseum, AA/A Kouprianoff; **157** Keukenhof, AA/M Jourdan; **158** Bos, AA/A Kouprianoff; **158/159** Bos, AA/A Kouprianoff; **160/161** Concertgebouw, AA/K Paterson; **162** Heineken Glass, AA/K Paterson; **163** Van Loon Museum, AA/M Jourdan; **166/167** Delftware, AA/K Paterson; **169** Delft, AA/K Paterson; The Hague, World Pictures; **173** Rotterdam, World Pictures; **174l** Utrecht, AA/A Kouprianoff; **174r** Pilsner bottles, AA/K Paterson; **177** Market, Pictures Colour Library; **178** Zandvoort, Alamy

Every effort has been made to trace the copyright holders, and we apologise in advance for any accidental errors. We would be happy to apply the corrections in the following edition of this publication.

Street Index

189

Dear Reader

Your comments, opinions and recommendations are very important to us. Please help us to improve our travel guides by taking a few minutes to complete this simple questionnaire.

You do not need a stamp (unless posted outside the UK). If you do not want to cut this page from your guide, then photocopy it or write your answers on a plain sheet of paper.

Send to: **The Editor, AA World Travel Guides, FREEPOST SCE 4598, Basingstoke RG21 4GY.**

Your recommendations...

We always encourage readers' recommendations for restaurants, nightlife or shopping – if your recommendation is used in the next edition of the guide, we will send you a **FREE AA Guide** of your choice from this series. Please state below the establishment name, location and your reasons for recommending it.

_____

_____

_____

_____

_____

Please send me **AA Guide** _____

About this guide...

Which title did you buy?

AA _____

Where did you buy it? _____

When? <u>m m</u> / <u>y y</u>

Why did you choose this guide? _____

_____

_____

_____

Did this guide meet your expectations?

Exceeded ☐   Met all ☐   Met most ☐   Fell below ☐

Were there any aspects of this guide that you particularly liked? _____

_____

_____

continued on next page...

Is there anything we could have done better? _____
_____
_____
_____

About you...
Name (*Mr/Mrs/Ms*) _____
Address _____
_____
_____ Postcode

Daytime tel nos _____
Email _____

Please only give us your mobile phone number or email if you wish to hear from us about
other products and services from the AA and partners by text or mms, or email.

Which age group are you in?
Under 25 ☐   25–34 ☐   35–44 ☐

How many trips do you make a year?
Less than one ☐   One ☐   Two ☐

Are you an AA member? Yes ☐   No ☐

About your trip...
When did you book? m m / y y

How long did you stay? _____

Was it for business or leisure? _____

Did you buy any other travel guides for yo

If yes, which ones? _____
_____

Thank you for taking the time to complete
possible, and remember, you do not need

| **AA** Travel Insurance call 0800